DISCLOSURE 101

What You Need To Know

Edition 07/04/14

I0429180

Contents

Note

This book is an adaptation of an email I received from my friend — Anna von Reitz — that included five pdf documents which supplemented her email with information that every red blooded American should know.

I accepted Anna's offer to get hard copies of this information into the hands of Americans.

I find it much to my advantage to have hard copy information to highlight and read without sitting at a computer for hours on end.

I hope you will find this hard copy presentation an advantage as well.

David E. Robinson
The Maine Patriot
Brunswick, Maine

http://maine-patriot.com

Preface

*the <u>continental</u> United States of America
is NOT the <u>district</u> United States of America*

— — —

Here's a series of revealing questions from a **court attack case** — just change **"james-thomas:mcbride"** to *your* name, and it's all the same.

Does this Court have any information or documentation proving otherwise?

I am giving you the whole story to pass on. Don't fail me. Somehow print it out, email it, **get hard copies into the hands of Americans** — and always remember that **you are an American State Citizen**, not a **"US citizen"**.

Each and every one of you has more civil authority on the land than the entire "federal government". You must learn to exercise that power with a sure hand, indeed, as "kings" and "queens" without subjects.

Anna von Reitz

"Let the unlearned learn, and the learned delight in remembering."

Introduction

I was 16, working my first job as a waitress in an old fashioned country diner. For some reason I don't recall, I was home one afternoon watching C-Span.

They were covering the confirmation hearings for Nelson Rockefeller to be confirmed as Gerald Ford's VP. The question was asked of him how much money he made the prior year. He answered something like '$480 million' and then he was asked how much federal income tax he paid on that amount, and he said he hadn't paid any income tax. Stunned silence. Do you mean to say that you received $480 million dollars in income last year and you paid no federal income tax at all? Nelson repeated — none. And that was that. The conversation shifted and went on to other topics. I knew right then that something was terribly wrong. The rest of the story is all about learning the details.

We got off track in the 1860 elections. Abraham Lincoln was a member of the Bar Association and not eligible to serve as President of The United States of America (major). So they ran him for the office of "President" of the United States — a private commercial company — and just didn't bother to explain the difference to the people. When he subsequently entered the "The United States (Company)" into bankruptcy on April 24, 1863, he handed our future over to European central banking interests and to the British Crown. His efforts to repair that error eventually led to his murder.

So there's the "President" and there's the "President" — one the leader of a nation, and one the CEO of a commercial company. What is going on here? Duplicity, obviously. And semantic deceit.

The entire fraud against the American States and American State Citizens relies upon men wearing many different "hats" at the same time, and exercising those offices — often in direct conflict of interest with each other — at the same time.

It also depends on immense amounts of semantic deceit via the use of similar names.

The United States that Lincoln entered into bankruptcy was not the American nation, or even a union of states. It was a **commercial company** formed by Ben Franklin in 1754, a **privately owned and operated commercial company** that received all the juicy governmental services contracts explicitly described as the **"nineteen enumerated Powers"** delegated to this new company — plus, the responsibility to oversee and manage and protect The United States Trust (1789).

If you look up the ***original*** equity contract establishing the "federal" government, you will see that it is called **"The Constitution for the united States of America"** and that it is a two part document. The first part, the **Preamble**, is a trust indenture that was later supplemented by the **Bill of Rights**. The second part is a **governmental services contract**. The United States (Company) that Franklin started and that Lincoln bankrupted was an odd blend of **Trust Management Organization** (TMO) and **governmental services company**.

All successors to that original contract have similarly been charged with the responsibility of **protecting** the national trust and **providing** governmental services.

After the Civil War we went through **"reconstruction"** — also known as **bankruptcy reorganization** — and a new **Trust Management Organization** was formed doing business as the **United States of America, Incorporated**. This entity was chartered by the Roman Catholic Church in Delaware as a **religious non-profit organization**. It was purchased by the

Federal Reserve Banks in 1912, run into the ground, and bankrupted in 1933. This time, the goons operating the "federal" government moved to implement a giant **Reverse Trust Scam** aimed at the assets of **The United States Trust** (1789).

FDR did this by claiming that the American States and American State Citizens were voluntary **"sureties"** backing the debts of **"the United States of America, Inc."** This gave the European bankers the excuse needed to **"hypothecate"** maritime liens against the property and assets of the American States and the American State Citizens. **Hypothecation is a means of stealthy theft**, similar to what happens when you agree to co-sign a car loan. A lien is established against your property, but the lien isn't exercised as long as the **"person"** you co-signed for pays his bills on time.

FDR volunteered us to stand good for credit extended to **"the United States of America, Inc."** and its **"secondaries"** in bankruptcy. The process of hypothecation allows the bank to establish a title claim against real properly without the necessity of physically obtaining the title, so nobody knew the difference. We were all **assumed** to agree to this because we didn't speak up and object, but then, we could hardly object to a contract if we didn't know that it existed, could we?

In 1944, FDR quit claimed all the assets and liabilities of **"the United States of America, Inc."** to the International Monetary Fund, an agency of the UN. The IMF set up yet **another** Trust Management Company calling itself the **UNITED STATES (INC.)** to administer the juicy federal service contracts while **"the United States of America, Inc."** was in Chapter 11 Reorganization.

As of July 1, 2013, **the United States of America, Inc.,** which was owned and operated by the FEDERAL RESERVE, which in turn was newly chartered under the "United Nations" — a separate independent city state operating on our shores — **was**

released from bankruptcy.

All debts were settled and discharged. This means that the IMF d.b.a. the UNITED STATES can no longer charge us and the several states for government services — quite aside from the fact that it was all fraud to begin with and they never should have **"presumed"** us to be sureties at all. Now the IMF must get "us" to re-contract with it, while the FEDERAL RESERVE is attempting to assert its prior right to the service contracts.

Central to all this fraud is the process of **'re-venuing'** — where the lawyers **redefine** you and your natural estate as "THINGS" — as "legal fiction entities" — to better plunder your assets.

Most recently, you were presumed "dead, missing at sea" and your ESTATE trust (a Roman Inferior Trust) was **"removed"** to Puerto Rico. These ESTATE trusts, named after living Americans, do business in NAMES styled like, JOHN QUINCY ADAMS, and they are all forced to function under the maritime jurisdiction of Puerto Rico — a Commonwealth member of a consortium of **"American states"** including Guam, American Samoa, the State of New Columbia (DC), and entities more commonly thought of as **"federal territories and possessions"** — but functioning as a separate nation calling itself **"the United States of America"** (minor).

You've been presumed to be legally dead all of your life. You've been presumed to be voluntarily employed as a caretaker of your own estate (for free) and a chattel thereof. Thus the rats have contrived to cheat the beneficiaries of **The United States Trust** (1789) subject to the whims of the **"US CONGRESS"** and have contrived to beat them out of their natural inheritance and to subject them to peonage and "debt slavery" caused by the enforced use of "notes"— that is, I.O.U's — instead of money.

"Notes" are not money. Notes are a means of conveying

never ceasing debt. This is the scam that has been used to force everyone in America to "accept" worthless paper **"in equitable exchange"** for real assets.

Now, once again, the same old scam is being set up. The IMF's franchise d.b.a. UNITED STATES, INC. is being prepared for bankruptcy. Mr. Obama has run its credit beyond the hilt, and just as the Federal Reserve bankrupted "the United States of America, Inc." in 1933 and pretended that we and our property were all sureties "standing good" for its debts, the IMF will pretend that all the Puerto Rican ESTATE trusts are "legal" assets belonging to it, ready for the picking of its creditor — the "UNITED NATIONS".

So as the UNITED STATES, INC. prepares to go bankrupt, all your ESTATES are being "redefined" and "revenued" again — this time, you are supposed to be transmitting utilities operating under names styled like this: "JOHN Q. PUBLIC" — owned and operated by the UNITED NATIONS and subject to its "laws" and the whims of its directors.

If you don't vehemently object, and directly to Secretary General Ki-Ban Moon, and to Pope Francis, and to the US POSTMASTER GENERAL, and put your feet down by the millions, they will get away with this **gratuitous fraud** against you and your States and your private assets once again.

Spread the word and make it count. Stomp on the toes of those pretending to be "your" representatives in the US Congress and tell them that they have done you a gross disservice and breached both trust and contract. Hold them accountable for this mess. **HOLD THEM ALL ACCOUNTABLE.** Tell them that they have **criminally** mismanaged The United States Trust (1789) and you will not pay for the fraud practiced against you and will not honor any of the agreements made **"in your behalf"** by these false representatives since December 31, 1865 — the day that the **original Republic** ceased to function as a nation.

This situation is nothing less than attempted **Identity Theft** of an entire nation and its people. It cannot be allowed to stand. Let the world see that we have been overtaken by **criminals**. Let it be firmly understood that they do **NOT** represent the American State nor the American State Citizens.

Anna von Reitz

1
Nothing Ever Changes, Until We Do...

Nothing Ever goes quite the way we plan in life, does it? I just wanted to be a nerdy scientist, but instead . . . there are many reasons why my favorite prophet is Jeremiah. Our times are so like his. We have the opportunity to choose the right things. But *will* we?

One day as I was reading some old arcane public documents when it all just clicked into place. I realized how our country and our government have been usurped by foreign powers and that African Americans were never really set free, and that, instead, the rest of us have been enslaved too, and I could not rest. Like everyone else, I felt overwhelmed, uncertain, at a loss — what to do? I am just one person. And my husband is just one person. And each one of you is "just one person".

The long trail from there led me to Rome and back, through every dusty by-way. Now I am forwarding some very important documents to you and entrusting you to get them distributed to members of the church, the armed services, your family, veterans, immigrants, retirees, and any African American who cares about freedom — REAL freedom — for ALL of us at last.

It's a complex story spanning 150 years, but it isn't all that hard to understand. Just look at the history and learn . . . after the Civil War, black Americans were only given *"US citizenship"* and *"civil rights"* — not the *"Natural and Unalienable rights"* they are heir to. Instead, the rotten *"government"* turned around and claimed the *"former"* slaves as chattel backing US government debt. Slavery didn't end. **It just shifted from *private* slave ownership to the *public* ownership of slaves.**

Gradually, the perpetrators (banks and lawyers) contrived to impose this new kind of *"commercial slavery"* on nearly everyone. They did this by stealth, fraud, undisclosed contract, false representation, you name it, they did it, but the basic scam was this:

Agencies hired by foreign banks (The Federal Reserve) approached our Mothers under the pretense of being legitimate government agencies having a mandate to *"record"* our **birth**. Instead, they registered our *"berth"* — they claimed to be in receipt of a *"foreign situs" trust* similar to what a harbormaster does when a ship docks — and they used this deceit to claim that we disappeared while owing a large amount of money to the Federal Reserve — *"missing; presumed lost at sea"* — and attached *maritime salvage liens* to our estates. Crazy as this seems, this is what they did as a device to lay claim to our assets. In this way, undeclared foreign agents of a foreign for-profit corporation obtained *false claims against us* in international jurisdictions of the law. Our estates were probated before most of us ever left the cradle.

Everything we have, everything we are, is presumed to be part of our *"estate"*. It was rolled over into another kind of *"trust"* by the probate court — a **Roman Inferior Trust** and that trust was *"re-venued"* to Puerto Rico and the jurisdiction of the **the district United States** — *the Union of American states* composed of *the State of New Columbia (DC), Puerto Rico, Guam, American Samoa, American Virgin Islands,* and *et alia* — *the "Seven Insular (meaning island) States"*. You see: it is all fraud, all built on semantic deceit and *"similar names"*.

Here's a series of revealing questions from a **court attack case** — just change **"james-thomas:mcbride"** to *your* name, and it is all the same.

Our records similarly show that **james-thomas** brought claim for his life before the Holy See after unscrupulous men deprived him of his natural estate while still a baby in his cradle. These individuals falsely claimed that they *"represented"* him, claimed that *their* commercial corporation was his beneficiary, misappropriated his credit, seized his estate, and enslaved him [**and likewise, you**] as chattel belonging to his [**your**] own estate, without his [**your**] knowledge or consent. Thereafter, they claimed that he was an *employee* of their corporation, a **"volunteer"** performing various jobs including work as a postal union employee, a merchant mariner, a withholding agent for the collection of taxes, and other duties as assigned, *without payment* or other consideration for this work. **Does this Court have any information or documentation proving otherwise?**

It is our understanding that *there are 2 entities* calling themselves the *united states of America* and they are (1) *the continental United States of America* — *the 50 geographical states* created by *statehood compacts* or *commonwealth trusts* joined together by *The Articles of Confederation (1781),* — and (2) *the district United States of America* — *the Union of American states,* a.k.a. *the federal zone UNITED STATES* — *the 7 Insular states* owned by *the 50 geographical states* as *federal territories* and *possessions,* including *the State of New Columbia (DC)/ Puerto Rico/ Guam/ American Samoa/ American Virgin Islands/* and *et alia.*

Does *any* Court have information or documentation proving otherwise?

According to *our records* as part of the fraud perpetuated against **james-thomas:mcbride** and his estate — his estate was **re-venued** (*revenued*) twice — once by a corporate franchise of *THE UNITED STATES INC.* doing business under conditions of semantic deceit and again by the *INTERNATIONAL MONETARY FUND* (IMF) doing business as *THE UNITED STATES INC.* which removed *his estate* [and your estate] to Puerto Rico and the foreign jurisdiction of *the federal zone UNITED STATES* described above. **Does any Court have information or documentation proving otherwise?**

I am giving you the whole story to pass on. Don't fail me. Somehow print it out, email it, get hard copies into the hands of Americans — and always remember that **you are an American State Citizen**, not a **"US citizen"**.

Each and every one of you has more civil authority on the land than the entire "federal government". You must learn to exercise that power with a sure hand, indeed, as "kings" and "queens" without subjects.

For those of you who are lawyers, I do not hold you in contempt. The rats had you over a barrel, too. Now that *the "Bar licenses" to act as privateers are extinguished* (Pope Francis's **Motu Proprio** dated July 11, 2013, effective **September 1, 2013**) you too, can make new choices and choose to live in a different world.

The actions disclosed in these documents are all on the public record. Taken together they describe nothing less than the **identity theft** of the entire nation known as The United States of America (major). It was done by the Lords of the Admiralty (Winston Churchill), FDR (who double-crossed them in the end), the Bar Association, the CIA, and three rogue organizations in addition to the corporations running the *UNITED NATIONS,* the *IMF,* and the *FEDERAL RESERVE* — these three holding companies have absorbed *AS CREDIT* — the entirety of the so-called *"National Debt"*. They did this via manipulation of the **fiat** *debt-credit* **monetary system**.

Here are the details of the "Debtors":

THE FEDERAL RESERVE SYSTEM, 20th Street NW, Washington, DC 20551, Organizational Number AG59880464

A U.S.S.E.C, a trust under 15 USC, is holding $15 trillion owed to "your" ESTATES.

E PLURIBUS UNUM - THE UNITED STATES OF AMERICA, 1500 Pennsylvania Avenue NW, Washington, DC 20220, AG59880464 A.

U.S. DEPARTMENT OF DEFENSE - FINANCE AND ACCOUNTING SERVICES, 1400 Defense Pentagon, Washington, DC 20310-1400.

They set this whole mess up as a *"generational skipping trust"* so that you never realize any benefit. The false *"trustees"* who are in gross breach of trust, all international banks who are operating these agencies, have instead siphoned off the credit owed to you via their **Reverse Trust Scam**. Generation after generation, they glut off the work and creativity and resources of the living people and the land, growing richer while their victims grow poorer.

I love you, my friends. In undertaking this work I have done it free-willingly. I was born on June 6 and I can never turn my back on the boys who stormed ashore on Normandy, nor on JFK — who was also born on June 6, and who was murdered while trying to expose and correct this same horrifying travesty. Whatever happens, I am "just" one person, but so was Jesus and so was Gandhi — and so, dear ones, are you!

2

The Real History

The Birth Certificate Trust: JOHN QUINCY PUBLIC ("Federal") Vessel in Commerce — the "person" recorded by "your" Birth Certificate — is created by Washington, DC Statute. Vital Statistics Chapter 2, Sec 7-201, paragraph 10, identifies *the "person" using your given name* as that federal municipal trust.

The nature of this trust is a **Roman Inferior Trust**, a.k.a. *Cestui Que Vie* Trust. It was ordered to be created by the Secretary of the Treasury of Puerto Rico, the Bankruptcy Trustee in charge of the bankruptcy of the **"United States of America, Incorporated"**, *a failed governmental services corporation* chartered in Delaware by the Roman Catholic Church, the church that FDR was "President" of, having no legitimate claim on **any** property belonging to **any** of the American states formed by Statehood Compacts — that is, REAL geographically defined "states".

We, the living Americans, were — as a result of the acts of the "US Bankruptcy Trustee" — declared dead, missing, presumed lost at sea, on the *"sea" of commerce*. Proof of this is found in Classification of *"infant/decedent"* in the Internal Revenue Manual - IRM 21.7.13.3.2.3 "infant/decedent". When we notify the IRS of our corrected status as *living* instead of the *"infant/decedent"* and assign *reversionary interest* in the SS trust/estate to and for the account of the United States, Title 12 USC 95(a)(2) and 12 USC 95(b) for *"full acquittance and discharge"* of *"all"* debts, we will be free of IRS control.

This is the remedy guaranteed to us as a result of the

US Congress issuing fiat *"debt notes"* based on our labor; however, the vast majority of us never agreed to this "new deal" and retain *full right of ownership and claim* to our assets. We are owed the **"re-venue"** of our property **without** signing away any of our prerogatives and rights. The **"peace offer"** from the criminals running the **"US" Congress** is only a means for the perpetrators of crimes to avoid the consequences of their acts by presumably securing our consent and a *presumptive commercial contract* allowing their abuse and our own enslavement to continue.

The United States of America (**minor**) never had any right to create **the JOHN QUINCY PUBLIC Trust** in the first place. So all assets of **the Roman Inferior Trusts** revert to the entitlement holder, and must be returned to the entitlement holder (*"re-venued"*) free of encumbrances and debt accumulated by any false trustees or secondary beneficiaries.

Once it is clear that we are acting as *living Americans* (and we are) and not agreeing to act as *incorporated "things"*, all members of the American Bar Association are *obligated* by the very Treaty that allows their presence on our soil *to lend "aid and assistance" to us and all members of the United States of America* (**major**)*, and the military forces are obligated to come to our defense.* So unless you work for the Puerto Rican Commonwealth, and hope to be paid by them, you'd all better make tracks on the right track.

The Social Security Trust: John Quincy Public (State) Vessel in Commerce

The Social Security Trust was created by the Social Security Act of 1935. It says what it says. It is bogus and coercive, based on fraud by criminals, unfunded except by the labor and contributions of its victims.

20

Article 31 and Article 38 of the Lieber Code, General Order 100:

31. Holding Title in Abeyance — all property held in abeyance — including the baby born on the battlefield and the income stream from that "asset". **DoD** takes the property "in trust" to hold in "abeyance" *for "safekeeping"*.

38. Issuance of "Indemnification Receipt" — the Birth Certificate. As peaceful civilian inhabitants we are *"indemnified" from any damage resulting from the actions of the US Army.*

Only *peaceful, living inhabitants* of the Domestic and organic states have the **civil authority** to command the Armed Forces of The United States of America (**major**). **Only *we* can require the "US Congress" and the "President" of a governmental services corporation under contract to serve us to quit their criminal shenanigans or be ousted like vermin chased from a storehouse.**

All others, including President Obama, by accepting the *"citizenship"* of *the corporate UNITED STATES,* have given up their right to say anything whatsoever to our military forces. The legitimate Armed Forces of *the corporate UNITED STATES* — the Seven Insular "States" existing as *federal territories* and *possessions* — includes the whole **Puerto Rican Navy** and whatever security forces are endemic to Guam, American Samoa, et alia.

3

Final Notice of Commercial and Adminitrative Default

February 3, 2014

Dana Fabe, Chief Justice
US Certified Mail # 7012 2210 0000 2447 3821

Alaska Judicial Council
US Certified Mail #7012 2210 0000 2447 3753

Alaska Attorney General
US Certified Mail # 7012 2210 0000 2447 3760

Governor Sean Parnell
US Certified Mail # 7012 2210 0000 2447 3777

Lt. Governor Mead Treadwell
US Certified Mail # 7012 2210 0000 2447 3784

US marshal Robert Huen
US Certified Mail # 7012 2210 0000 2447 3791

Colonel Jim Cockerell, Alaska State Troopers
US Certified Mail # 7012 2210 0000 2447 3845

Ms. Betsy Lawer, CEO, First National Bank of Alaska
US Certified Mail #7012 2210 0000 2447 3814

Joseph Everheart, Regional President
301 West Northern Lights Blvd, Anchorage, AK 99501
US Certified Mail # 7012 2210 0000 2447 3883

Abstract: Since 1944 the International Monetary Fund (IMF) an **agency of the UNITED NATIONS** doing business as the **UNITED STATES, INC.** d.b.a. **STATE OF ALASKA** has functioned as a secondary Trust Management Organization (TMO) charged with the fiduciary obligation of fulfilling **all** service contracts of the bankrupted **United States of America, Incorporated**, during its Chapter 11 reorganization. In accepting the **assets** of the United States of America, Inc. the IMF also accepted its **liabilities**, which include the **claims of the Priority Creditors;** living Americans who are owed:

(1) reparations for the seizure of privately owned gold assets by the United States of America, Inc. acting in Breach of Trust during the 1930's,

(2) all interest in their private property, material rights, land, homes, businesses, persons and names that have been improperly entangled in the bankruptcy of the privately owned "United States of America, Incorporated" and

(3) the **natural resources** possessed by the organic, geographically defined states of the Union.

The IMF has claimed to represent the interests of all the Creditors of the United States of America, Inc., but has instead alleged that the living American People — to whom the IMF and its many subsidiaries owe good faith service — are "unknown creditors". Chronic abuse by the IMF leadership and politicians acting in conflict of interest as corporate officers and employees of this privately owned and operated for-profit corporation d.b.a. the UNITED STATES, INC. — at the same time that they claim to "represent" the American People, has led to unrestrained and unauthorized hypothecation of public debt against private assets, identity theft, fiduciary malfeasance, fraud, extortion under armed force, and Breach of Trust usurpation.

You are receiving this FINAL NOTICE OF COMMERCIAL AND ADMINISTRATIVE DEFAULT because you work for the UNITED NATIONS/IMF d.b.a.

the **UNITED STATES, INC. or one of its STATE franchises or agencies, or a banking institution impacted by these facts.** You are responsible in some capacity for meeting the contractual and fiduciary obligations owed to the American People. **You are being made explicitly, individually, personally, and undeniably aware of criminal acts of mis-administration and malfeasance being committed and directed by IMF corporate officers functioning in blatant Breach of Trust and Conflict of Interest while occupying vacated and long-inactive Public Offices.**

Absent a specific, <u>fully disclosed</u>, voluntary appointment to act in behalf of specific individual Americans, there is no basis for any claim that any elected or appointed official employed by the UNITED STATES or its STATE franchises, agencies, or subsidiaries, represents anyone but themselves. Election to a corporate office does **not** imply Power of Attorney. Election to a private corporate office does **not** imply election to public office. The same is true of any elected or appointed official employed by the United States of America, Inc. and its State franchises.

Sean Parnell has been elected to serve as the GOVERNOR of the STATE OF ALASKA, a corporate municipal franchise of the UNITED STATES, INC. This is **not** the same office as the **Alaska State Governor**, a civil office of the organic Alaska State.

The claims of the IMF d.b.a. UNITED STATES, INC. against the private property and Estates of the American People have been denied and successfully rebutted at the highest levels of world governance.

The "United States of America, Inc." has been released from bankruptcy as of July 1, 2013, and all debts related to it and its franchises have been discharged, so that the UNITED STATES, INC. cannot bill the United States of America, Inc. for services.

You are being afforded the opportunity to self-correct and correct the operations of your Office/OFFICE. Failure to timely do so and provide remedy to those who have been harmed may result in you being prosecuted for impersonating American officials, double indemnity fines, up to ten (10) years in prison for per offense, commercial compensatory damage claims, and dissolution of the IMF, franchise, agency, bank or other corporate charter of the legal fiction entity you work for.

NOTICE TO PRINCIPALS IS NOTICE TO AGENTS, NOTICE TO AGENTS IS NOTICE TO PRINCIPALS.

This letter is your COMPLETE AND FINAL NOTICE informing you of crimes being committed under the auspices of your Office/OFFICE, making you individually and personally liable, and serving to make everyone associated with your Office/OFFICE an accomplice to these continuing acts of criminal fraud and malfeasance if immediate action to correct operations is not taken.

America was founded under the administration of commercial **Trust Management Organizations**, the most famous of which was the Virginia Company. As a result of the Revolutionary War, the American People formed an **unincorporated domestic civil government**. The Several states later **contracted with** an **incorporated** Trust Management Organization d.b.a. "United States" to provide **international representation** and **stipulated public services** in common.

The American civil government based on individual and organic state sovereignty is known as The Republic. A more recent Trust Management Organization d.b.a. the United States of America,

Inc. clearly admitted its status as a mere representative of the Republic when it popularized the *Pledge of Allegiance*: "...and to the **Republic** *for which it stands*."

The Republic originally functioned in international commerce through the agency of an incorporated commercial Trust Management Organization known simply as the "United States". George Washington was the Eleventh President of this Trust Management Organization, which predated the Revolutionary War.

Thus there are two governments in America and there always have been. The **Republic**, which is the civil government of the American People, and a **Trust Management Organization** that is charged with providing nineteen enumerated services for the Sovereign States, most of which deal with international commerce.

The Republic States that entered into the original equity contract known as The Constitution for the united States of America were represented by the original Trust Management Company d.b.a. "United States" from 1789 to 1863 when it was entered into bankruptcy caused by the expense of the Civil War. A second Trust Management Organization called the "United States of America, Incorporated" functioned from 1871 to 1933. Thereafter, the United States of America, Inc. was entered into bankruptcy by Executive Order issued by its President, Franklin Delano Roosevelt. The United States of America, Incorporated, entered into the receivership of International Bankruptcy Trustees, specifically, the Secretary of the Treasury of Puerto Rico, selected by the Creditors — the IBRD, World Bank, and Federal Reserve.

Since 1944, the United States of America, Incorporated's business affairs have been managed by these same international bankruptcy trustees under the direction of these same creditors organized as the International Monetary Fund (IMF) acting under various corporate names including the UNITED STATES, the UNITED STATES OF AMERICA, the USA, and E PLURIBUS UNUM THE UNITED STATES OF AMERICA.

The **State of Alaska** is a corporate municipal franchise of the bankrupted **United States of America, Incorporated**. The **STATE OF ALASKA** is a corporate municipal franchise of the **UNITED STATES, INCORPORATED**. These entities are **not** the same as the geographically defined **Alaska State**.

These Trust Management Organizations don't have a contract to operate the civil government, though they have been conniving and contriving to do so for several decades with disastrous results.

All bank officials operating businesses in the geographically defined Alaska State have knowingly or unknowingly set up checking, savings, and other depository accounts, including mortgage and escrow accounts, which result in **unlawful conversion of private property into corporate assets.** By creating these accounts in the **NAMES** of individual ESTATE trusts owned and operated by the UNITED STATES, INC. instead of the **names** of the living people, private bank accounts belonging to john-quincy:adams have been unlawfully converted to the ownership of Puerto Rican trusts owned and operated by the UNITED STATES, INC. under the NAME of JOHN QUINCY ADAMS.

This semantic deceit dependent upon the use of "similar names" and the constructive fraud of non-disclosure practiced by the banks has resulted in claims by the IMF d.b.a. UNITED STATES, INC. that the funds and contracts under deposit as negotiable instruments are the property of UNITED STATES, INC. "individual franchises" and are subject to seizure by the UNITED STATES, INC. and available to serve as collateral backing the debts of the UNITED STATES, INC.

All banks and bank officials operating in the Alaska State are under **NOTICE and DEMAND** to **correct** their records to reflect the fact that **all** assets contained in or claimed by "individual franchise ESTATE trusts" operated "in the name of" American Nationals and their private **unincorporated** business enterprises have been **redeemed** by the American Nationals having the same or similar given names and living at the geographic addresses of record on file.

All bank and bank officials operating in the Alaska State are under NOTICE that any claim presented by any officer of the UNITED STATES or the STATE OF ALASKA pretending an interest in the private property assets of American Nationals or seeking to withdraw deposits under the authority of the Dodd-Frank Act are prohibited from any such action by Public Law of the Republic, and that any bank complying with such demand will be <u>liquidated</u>. **Any banker aiding or abetting unlawful conversion of private assets for the benefit of the IMF d.b.a. UNITED STATES, INC. will be prosecuted to the fullest extent allowable under American Common Law.**

Any corporate Officer/OFFICER receiving this NOTICE who is unaware of the facts presented is invited to contact Interpol, the nearest Vatican Legate, or the International Services Agent for Alaska.

Any corporate Officer/OFFICER receiving this NOTICE who believes that we are misunderstanding any of the historical facts or any aspect of the material circumstance, is invited to produce the single document which they believe grants their agency or Office/OFFICE jurisdiction and/or controlling ownership interest in living Americans, their private property assets, their credit, their labor, their organic states or any other material assets.

In "representing" the Republic, the United States of America, Incorporated, was bound to honor all the contracts and Public Laws established by the Republic. In receivership, the United States of America, Incorporated, had to be operated according to the same Trust Indenture that was established by the Preamble and Bill of Rights, because it is not possible to receive the assets in bankruptcy without also receiving the liabilities. The UNITED STATES, INCORPORATED, acting as a secondary Trust

Management Organizaton since 1933 has in turn undertaken to "represent" the United States of America, Incorporated, and is bound by the **same** obligations.

We will address, briefly, the common claim made by Officers/ OFFICERS representing either the "United States of America, Inc." or the UNITED STATES, INC. to the effect that living American Nationals are "US citizens" subject to domination by any incorporated entity under contract to serve them.

According to the Act of the Republic enacted as Public Law by the Members of Congress Assembled as an unincorporated Body Politic of the Domestic States on April 14, 1802, (2 Stat. 153, c. 28, ss.1, Revised Statute 2165) — "an alien may be admitted to become a citizen of the United States in the following manner, **and not otherwise**."

This is Public Law fully enacted as substantive law by the **unincorporated** Body Politic operating under full commercial liability as the **domestic civil government** of the Several States. It cannot be amended or repealed by any "Act" of any incorporated Trust Management Organization claiming to represent the Republic, and it sets forth a lengthy process that is required to redefine any American National as a "US citizen" subject to the corporate jurisdiction of the United States of America, Inc. and/ or its Bankruptcy Trustees and successors, such as the UNITED STATES, STATE OF ALASKA, etc.

Any claim that any private contract entered into by individuals can magically overcome this prerequisite of Public Law stands mute and disproven by the entirety of the Federal Register and Code, which unfailingly describes American Nationals domiciled in the geographically defined organic states as "non-resident aliens" with respect to the United States of America, Inc. and its municipal jurisdiction.

Virtually no American Nationals have **ever** deliberately

undertaken to become "US citizens" as required by US Statute at Large 2. They have not by any knowing and voluntary act agreed to stand as sureties for a bankrupt Trust Management Organization calling itself the "United States of America" in 1930, 1933, 1959, or at any other time. They have not agreed under conditions of full disclosure to contract **at all** with the UNITED STATES, INC. to provide any services, much less have they granted any authorization to this foreign, privately-owned banking cartel to "represent" them or their interests as Priority Creditors of the United States of America, Inc.

They did not grant authorization to any Governor/ GOVERNOR or other elected or appointed official, corporate officer, employee, or hired contractor of the United States of America, Incorporated or the UNITED STATES, INCORPORATED, to represent them or their interests in these matters at any time from the founding of the Republic to date.

They did not under conditions of full disclosure voluntarily grant authorization allowing any Trust Management Company to operate public trusts under their individual names, to lay claim to their private assets by presumption under color of law, to hypothecate debt based upon the value of their labor, their homes, land, or other resources, or to otherwise impose the debts, statutes, codes, or regulations of any corporation upon them.

In 1995 a group of American Nationals moved to redeem and reclaim the individually named ESTATES created by the Secretary of the Treasury of Puerto Rico, the Bankruptcy Trustee appointed by the IMF. These Americans provided proof to the Internal Revenue Service/IRS and the Custodian of Alien Property/ CUSTODIAN OF ALIEN PROPERTY and the US Bankruptcy Trustees/US BANKRUPTCY TRUSTEES that they were alive and competent to administer their own affairs, and that they were Priority Creditors of the United States of America, Incorporated.

At that time and ever since, they have objected to any presumption that they are or ever were "wards of any State or STATE"—— ever incorporated, incompetent, or disabled.

They have uniformly declared and testified before the world that they have been defrauded, lied to, lied about, victimized by deliberate semantic deceit, suffered extortion, armed robbery, gross fiduciary malfeasance, inland piracy, conspiracy against their rights and material interests, have suffered from self-interested non-disclosure, breach of trust, despotism, and default of commercial contract—all at the hands of Trust Management Organizations that are **obligated** to function in good faith and with full fiduciary liability.

They have repudiated the claims of the United States of America, Inc. and the UNITED STATES, INC. which are merely privately owned for-profit commercial corporations no different than Microsoft, Incorporated, which have sought to attach the private property assets of individual American Nationals and the assets of the Republic via fraudulent deceit and misrepresentation. These Americans reclaimed their full sovereign authority among the nations of the world, and they redeemed all assets held in "public trusts" created by the United States of America, Inc. and the UNITED STATES, INC.

All debt accrued against any public trusts operated under the given names or variations thereof of American Nationals by the United States of America, Incorporated or the UNITED STATES, INCORPORATED and **any and all** incorporated franchises of these Trust Management Organizations — including the State of Alaska, STATE OF ALASKA, WELLS FARGO, INC., ABC MORTGAGE, INC, and so on — is to be discharged, dollar for dollar, without exception. Clear fee simple title to the assets is to be returned to the individual American Nationals and the organic states of the Republic.

The American Nationals have issued no valid proxy authorizing any agency, elected official, corporate officer, foreign agent or public employee of the United States of America, Inc. or the UNITED STATES, INC. to "represent" them in an abusive manner contrary to their material interests, nor did they grant any such authority to the Trust Management Organizations to represent them regarding these specific matters. **They recognize no claims brought against them, their private property assets, or their organic states which are based on representations made "in their behalf" by third parties acting in Breach of Trust and contract default.**

The leadership of the UNITED STATES, INC. known as the US CONGRESS has recently passed the Dodd/Frank Bill, gratuitously granting themselves the right to pillage the bank accounts of Americans which have been purposely and self-interestedly constructed by the IMF d.b.a. UNITED STATES, INC. as accounts belonging to federal franchise "ESTATE trusts" without the knowledge or consent of the victims.

The criminal intent of these actions is self-evident — first, to unlawfully convert private bank accounts to the ownership of "public trusts" owned and operated by for-profit corporations merely pretending to "represent" the victims, second, to claim that these private assets have been voluntarily "donated" to the public trust franchises, or "abandoned" by the legitimate beneficiaries of the assets.

This NOTICE is your individual passport to a real "federal" prison if you do not immediately cease and desist all participation in support of these claims, actions, and intents.

The living man, whose given name is properly written in this form: john-quincy:adams has been induced by undeclared foreign agents of the IMF d.b.a. UNITED STATES, INC. and the FEDERAL RESERVE d.b.a. United States of America, Inc. to believe that he is depositing his private property into his own private bank account, but in fact, he is always depositing his private property into a bank account owned by "John Quincy Adams" which is a *foreign situs* trust owned and operated by the United States of America, Inc. or "JOHN QUINCY ADAMS" which is an ESTATE trust owned by the banks operating the UNITED STATES, INCORPORATED.

Any Officer/OFFICER receiving this NOTICE who doubts that this is true is invited to pull out their "personal check book" and look at what appears to be the signature line under high magnification. You will see under high magnification that the line is not a line. It is a row of microprint endlessly repeating "authorizing signature" over and over. This verbiage has to be there, because the "owner" of the account, YOUR NAME, is a Puerto Rican Trust, and can't function without human agents.

The IMF, d.b.a. UNITED STATES, INC., has deceived millions of Americans into depositing their private assets into "public franchise accounts" without their knowledge or consent. Most likely many of the Officers/OFFICERS reading this NOTICE have been similarly victimized by this foreign interloper's deceit, fraud, and self-interest. To lead you along in this deception they have allowed you to write checks on "their" account and claimed that you are an employee of their corporation — and as such, required to obey all their "laws", rules, codes, statutes, and regulations that they may deem appropriate to establish and enforce.

This is all a form of **bunko** that has only been made possible because the banks operating as creditors gained a **position of trust** via the bankrupting of the Trust Management Organization dba the United States of America, Inc.

The IMF gained control of the apparatus of government services by creating the Secondary Trust Management Organization d.b.a. UNITED STATES, INC. which has been "filling in" while the United States of America, Inc. was in receivership. The FEDERAL RESERVE, another privately owned banking cartel, gained a similar position of trust as the primary creditor of the United States of America, Inc. throughout its bankruptcy reorganization.

The IMF d.b.a. UNITED STATES and its corporate OFFICERS and their appointed Bankruptcy Trustees commandeered the apparatus of what Americans mistakenly thought of as their government, claimed to "represent" the American People, and have gone on an eighty-year rampage of white collar fraud the likes of which has never been seen in the history of the world.

The IMF d.b.a. UNITED STATES, INC. has claimed that the American People have had a free choice in the midst of all this misrepresentation and unlawful conversion of assets. They could "redeem" their property held in the franchise ESTATE trusts set up in their NAMES by the banks at any time, simply by notifying the proper officials — the Internal Revenue Service.

The American Nationals were never told any of this, so this remedy was never actually made available in any practical sense to the millions of rank and file Priority Creditors of the United States of America, Inc.

The two Trust Management Organizations d.b.a. the United States of America, Inc. and the UNITED STATES, INC., were and are, both obligated to defend the National Trust, including the material interests and rights of individual Americans who are beneficiaries of the National Trust Indenture.

Breach of Trust results in severance of contract, including the service contracts that go along with the fiduciary obligations owed as liabilities of the IMF and its agencies and franchises to the living beneficiaries — the American Nationals.

Any concerted attempt by Trustees — whether individuals or entire vast incorporated Trust Management Organizations — to impose upon the beneficiaries of a trust or to usurp the assets and collateral held in trust for the Trustees or the Trust Manager's own benefit, is a **High Crime of Felony Fraud and Criminal Malfeasance.**

The Supreme Court for the State of Alaska/THE SUPREME COURT FOR THE STATE OF ALASKA and The Superior Court for the State of Alaska / THE SUPERIOR DISTRICT COURT FOR THE STATE OF ALASKA have been informed of these facts and have failed to correct their operations.

These Undeclared Foreign Agents and Agencies employed jointly by the FEDERAL RESERVE, a privately owned and operated Central Bank employed by the bankrupted "United States of America, Inc." and the IMF operating the UNITED STATES, INC., have continued to presume a controlling interest in the assets of individual American Nationals and in already-redeemed individual ESTATES and to also presume that the private property assets of individual Americans were offered as surety and collateral for debts owed by the "United States of America, Inc." — all based on insupportable and undocumented representations made by unauthorized third parties acting in Breach of Trust eighty years ago.

They have continued on this course knowingly and despite having their offers to contract refused and all these false presumptions thoroughly rebutted in individual court actions entered as demonstration cases: 3AN-12-6858CI and 3PA-12-1447CI.

This NOTICE includes presentation of <u>charges</u> against the Clerks and Judges operating The Superior District Court for the State of Alaska and the CLERKS and JUDGES operating THE SUPERIOR DISTRICT COURT FOR THE

STATE OF ALASKA.

If these Officers of the British Crown do not immediately cease and desist in their activities in support of the fraudulent misrepresentations and claims being made by their employers they will be subject to <u>deportation</u> and seizure of their individual property assets in Alaska.

This is your individual and personal NOTICE that not only are "Governors" of the "United States of America, Inc." and "GOVERNORS" of the "UNITED STATES" <u>not</u> authorized or empowered to pledge private property of any American National, they were never empowered to pledge any assets of the organic states, either.

All "Acts", pledges, agreements, and policies of the "US Congress" and "State Governors" operating the "United States of America, Inc." — a privately owned commercial corporation under contract to **serve** the Americans — and pretending to have affect upon living American Nationals, their private property assets, or their organic states is fraudulent, null and void as if these Acts never existed.

All "ACTS" of the "US CONGRESS" and "STATE GOVERNORS" operating the UNITED STATES, INC — a privately owned commercial corporation under contract to **serve** the Americans — and pretending to have affect upon living American Nationals, their private property assets, or their organic states is fraudulent, null and void as if these ACTS never were.

Similarly, all "legislative acts" of the State of Alaska and the STATE OF ALASKA operating as corporate municipal franchises of the "United States of America, Inc." or the "UNITED STATES, INC." which pretend to have affect upon Alaskans, their private property assets, or their organic state, are fraudulent, null and void as if they never were.

All rules, statutes, codes, regulations, taxes, tithes,

fees, penalties, and "laws" established by these corporations apply **only** to their employees and their corporate officers, similar to the **internal policies** set by any other commercial corporation on earth. Any pretension that any individual American National is obligated to obey these instruments of corporate policy as an "employee" must be backed up with proof of **fully disclosed** employment contracts and agreements.

This NOTICE informs you individually and personally that the individual living American Nationals, their private property, and their organic states, are <u>NOT subject to any law, statute, rule, code, regulation, order, or internal policy promulgated by any incorporated entity.</u>

THE SUPERIOR DISTRICT COURT FOR THE STATE OF ALASKA and the STATE OF ALASKA have been fully informed of these facts and have received and are right now receiving **direct instruction** from the actual **Entitlement Holders** regarding the status and proper administration of the individual Estates/ESTATES of Alaskans.

All corporate Officers/OFFICERS receiving this NOTICE now have **cause to know** that they **cannot rely** upon second-hand direction received from third parties merely claiming to "represent" individual Alaskans, nor claiming to have controlling interest in private assets held in public trusts that have been established "in the name of" individual Alaskans by the United States of America, Inc. and the UNITED STATES, INC.

All the individually named public trusts generated by the two Trust Management Organizations d.b.a. the United States of America, Inc. and the UNITED STATES, INC. are legal fictions which have been created under the auspices of the Holy See and the Roman Curia and **misused** as a means to plunder the private property assets of Americans and their organic states **under color of law.**

The persons promulgating, preserving, and supporting this abuse and fraud are criminals — outlaws on the land, and pirates on the sea. Anyone receiving this NOTICE who does not immediately cease and desist and correct their behavior, presumptions, and operations in whatever office they hold, is fully <u>liable</u>.

In "the name of" public trusts, the Trust Management Organizations pretending to represent the American states and individual living Americans have gone on compiling debts, creating bankruptcies, making false commercial claims, and otherwise seeking to ensnare and obligate assets of the US Trust for the benefit of their private shareholders for eighty years.

This is your <u>FINAL NOTICE</u> of these facts. You will be held individually and personally liable and accountable for any support of or continuing participation in these acts of fraud and breach of trust.

Members of the Bar Association who are by definition **citizens of the Inner City of London City State and foreigners on American soil** will be subject to deportation and seizure of all their private assets if they continue to presume against and impose upon the American Nationals who are their ultimate employers.

Corporate officers of the United States of America, Inc. or the UNITED STATES, INC. who continue to **impersonate** state judges or pretend to act as state civil officials, will be prosecuted to the fullest extent of the American Common Law if they do not voluntarily come into compliance and live within the limitations of their actual Office/OFFICE.

None of these Trust Management Organization schemes and actions — bankruptcies, debts, service contracts, etc. — have anything to do with any living American nor with any geographically defined state of the Union nor with any private assets belonging to these peaceful **<u>unincorporated</u>** entities, but through purposeful semantic deceit and fraud, false claims arising among these incorporated entities have been allowed to bleed over and impact the beneficiaries of the US Trust.

All of this uproar, all these claims and counter-claims, all these legal fiction entities battling it out with each other in corporate administrative tribunals, *have nothing whatsoever to do with the living people, their private assets or their organic states — and they never have had.*

The **only** business any living American National has with any corporate administrative tribunal functioning as a Court/COURT is . . .

(1) to inform the personnel operating the Court/COURT of facts pertaining to some issue being considered, or

(2) to present a claim against the United States of America, Inc. or the UNITED STATES, INC. or one of their franchises, such as the STATE OF ALASKA. See the Administrative Procedures Act of 1946 for statutory admission.

Beginning in 2009, American Nationals took their claims against the United States of America, Incorporated and the UNITED STATES, INCORPORATED — **both** — to the Holy See.

This is your individual and personal NOTICE that **all** authority to create legal fictions — trusts, public utilities, corporations, foundations, and cooperatives — derives directly and explicitly from the Holy See and from the law forms established and copyrighted by the Roman Curia.

Along with the power to create comes the power to destroy.

The Holy See has the power and the right to dissolve the UNITED NATIONS Charter, the IMF Charter, the UNITED STATES Charter, and so on, *ad infinitum*, to order the distribution of the assets of these legal fiction entities to their creditors, and the Pope has the additional unlimited ability to rewrite or void any "law" created by any **incorporated** entity worldwide.

In 2010 Pope Benedict XVI agreed with the American Nationals that gross Breach of Trust and fiduciary malfeasance related to the administration of the US National Trust and the individually named public trusts has occurred.

Remedy begun in 2010 has been continued by Pope Francis d.b.a. FRANCISCUS, acting as CEO of the Global Estate Trust.

This correction is coming directly from the Highest Contracting Powers, from the very top of the interlocking trust directorate that has incorporated virtually all the Trust Management Organizations responsible for administering government services worldwide — including *both* the United States of America, Incorporated, and the UNITED STATES, INCORPORATED.

Private attorneys and civil postmasters and international diplomatic agents in every organic state of the Union have been appointed either directly by the Holy See or under the Holy See's direction to communicate these facts to all those responsible for the administration of the Trust Management Organizations and their franchises and agencies responsible for the deplorable conditions of abuse, fraud, and criminality engulfing America.

This is your <u>FINAL NOTICE</u>: The legal fiction organizations you work for will be liquidated if they do not come into compliance and function lawfully.

Demonstration court cases have been prosecuted in Alaska seeking to re-educate those who are individually responsible for administration of the respective Trust Management Organizations, their franchises, and agencies. Every good faith effort has been made to provide discussion and bring the recipients of this NOTICE to their senses, to avoid the necessity of dissolving corporate charters and forcing arrests, but clearly, correction must be made and it must be done with alacrity to avoid further damage to the American Nationals and their organic states.

Case Number 3AN-12-6858CI was prosecuted **entirely** via Special Appearance — **by definition,** merely to **inform** THE SUPERIOR DISTRICT COURT FOR THE STATE OF ALASKA.

The COURT pretended to have jurisdiction it didn't have, grossly misrepresented its authority, willfully concealed its actual nature, function, and role, failed to require validated proof of an international commercial claim, failed to require identification of the true parties of interest, failed to require proof of ownership and provenance of an unregistered Promissory Note, pretended to misunderstand clearly enunciated statements denying consent and claims of identity, and pretended to have authority to seize private property assets under Federal Debt Collection Procedures though no viable public trusts, federal or State, were even in evidence. Officers of the COURT d.b.a. JERMAIN, DUNNAGAN, and OWENS in the person of MICHELE BOUTIN, ESQ. hired the ALASKA STATE TROOPERS to trespass on private property and to extort over $100,000.00 USD under armed force.

Confronted with the facts, THE SUPREME COURT FOR THE STATE OF ALASKA failed to take appropriate corrective action and instead acted as an accomplice to the errors and crimes committed.

Another case 3PA-12-1447CI was similarly prosecuted. After voluminous correspondence with the COURT, the MATANUSKA-SUSITNA BOROUGH, and the respective political officials, someone, somewhere, bowed to the simple truth — that the MATANUSKA-SUSITNA BOROUGH is a franchise of the STATE OF ALASKA which is a franchise of the UNITED STATES, INC. which is providing services based on fraudulent misrepresentation and without a valid contract, and then demanding payment and alleging a security interest in private property that isn't theirs. The MATANUSKA-SUSITNA BOROUGH foreclosure action was dropped and the supposed "tax debt" erased from the books, but the next year they attempted to repeat the same errors and commit the same acts of mis-administration and malfeasance.

The "United States of America, Inc." and the UNITED STATES, INC. are both commercial corporations — privately and mostly foreign-owned commercial corporations. They have no special standing at all. With respect to American Nationals they have precisely the same standing as any other multi-national corporate conglomerate.

This is your NOTICE of the facts. These incorporated entities can't force individual American Nationals to accept services, buy insurance, pay taxes, or do anything else based on the representations of third parties merely claiming to represent them. They have no authority to arrest, imprison, or detain any American National for any "crime" lacking a *corpus delecti* demonstrating actual harm to other living people or their property. If they persist in providing services without a valid contract, they have no recourse to complain if they don't get paid and no enforceable security interest in private property.

The American People are accommodating these Trust Management Organizations and paying them to provide stipulated government services, <u>not the other way around</u>. It should not be necessary for individual Americans to prosecute law suits simply to secure the proper administration of long-standing fiduciary obligations from their <u>*employees and service vendors.*</u>

Consider carefully the consequences of continuing to mis-administer the public trusts and using these deceptively named commercial vessels as an excuse to plunder the private property assets of the American People. **Piracy, including inland piracy, is a crime.** As of **September 1, 2013**, each corporate officer, each hired administrator, is **individually liable**, from the "President of the UNITED STATES" on down to the lowliest clerk.

The United States, Canada, Australia, England, Ireland, Scotland, New Zealand, South Africa — have all been similarly victimized by international bankers and the self-serving and/or ignorant politicians who have betrayed the interests of the people they claim to represent.

These countries all stand to be devastated by a struggle to force the politicians, administrators, bankers and jurists responsible for this mess to . . .

(1) get their hands out of other people's pockets,

(2) do their actual jobs,

(3) stop making insupportable claims against private property assets that **don't** belong to the corporations they work for, and

(4) refuse to execute unlawful "orders" received from the "President" of a corporation that has exactly the same relationship with respect to American Nationals as the President of J.C. PENNY or the President of SOUTHWEST AIR, INC.

In one capacity or another, you are all responsible for oversight and administration of the Trust Management Organizations involved in this national-scale debacle. You all have cause to know what the truth is and to act accordingly. There should be no doubt in your minds that the fiduciary obligations described herein exist and that the contracts creating and protecting the **National Trust Indenture** will be honored — even if it requires armed intervention, arrests, and liquidation of the world's largest financial institutions.

Undeclared Foreign Agents have operated the Alaska Court System / ALASKA COURT SYSTEM and The Superior District

Court for the State of Alaska / THE SUPERIOR DISTRICT COURT FOR THE STATE OF ALASKA in an stubbornly criminal and fraudulent manner in violation of their corporate charter, resulting in false claims of jurisdiction, grand felony acts of armed extortion and inland piracy, fiduciary malfeasance, constructive fraud, unlawful conversion, and numerous other crimes including assaults against unarmed American civilians.

In 3AN-12- 6858CI THE SUPERIOR DISTRICT COURT FOR THE STATE OF ALASKA employed all the fraud gambits described herein, including grossly over-stepping its jurisdiction. THE SUPERIOR DISTRICT COURT FOR THE STATE OF ALASKA, INC. owes the private estate trust pillaged in that matter over $400,000.00 USD times (4) four as compensatory damages. Until that debt is paid and restitution to the individual American Nationals made, the STATE OF ALASKA is in Breach of Trust and Contract Default increasing the Public Debt, in violation of its Corporate Charter, and is **subject to dissolution**. A complete bounty collection of $50,000,000.00 USD may additionally be applied against the State of Alaska, Inc. for violation of XIV Section 4 of its Charter.

This is your individual and personal NOTICE that failure to stop crime, like failure to make every reasonable effort to prevent crime, makes you an accomplice to the crime. You are liable. You have been fully informed. This NOTICE has been <u>recorded</u> worldwide. Failure to render assistance and provide remedy to the victims of crime also makes you an accomplice to the crime.

Criminality of the kind described herein and failure to honor contractual and fiduciary duties owed is due cause for severance of your contract for services, criminal prosecution, and dissolution of the corporations you work for. Cease and desist all improper actions.

This NOTICE is by my hand and upon my civil authority set this _____ day of February, 2014:

Anna Maria Wilhelmina Hanna Sophia Riezinger-von Reitzenstein von Lettow-Vorbeck, Private Attorney in Service to His Holiness, Pope Francis
In Care Of: Box 520994, Big Lake, Alaska
Under Sea

4

Final Judgment and Civil Orders

<u>**APRIL 11, 2014**</u>

For Example:

When you applied for a "marriage license" a private, for-profit franchise of the UNITED NATIONS doing business as the STATE OF_____ claimed a custodial **ownership** interest in your marital relationship and the products resulting from it. On the basis of your own signature, this entity secretively claimed to own you, your wife, and your children as chattel. According to them, when you apply for a marriage license, the nature of the marriage contract changes and becomes a "civil contract".

"Marriage is a civil contract to which there are three parties - the husband, the wife and the state." — *Van Koten v. Van Koten. 154 N.E. 146.*

Did you ever *intend* to give a foreign privately owned corporation merely calling itself the STATE OF_____ permission to distribute your assets in a divorce, to force you to pay alimony and child support, or to seize custody of your minor children under armed force?

Were these results of signing a "marriage license" ever disclosed to you by the STATE? Did the STATE disclose its identity and nature, as a franchise of a foreign, for-profit, privately owned corporation?

You were *never* required to have a marriage license, to be lawfully married — but was that fact ever fully disclosed to you by the STATE? We think not.

You have the absolute right to rescind your signature from any contract that was not fully disclosed to you. Such a contract is null and void, as if it never existed at all, and all payments and other asset distributions exercised under it are subject to return to the lawful owner(s), plus reasonable interest.

You are *not* obligated by any contract obtained under conditions of fraud, deceit, or non-disclosure. The STATE is culpable for its failure to disclose.

Any demand that you produce a **"marriage license"** as a prerequisite to access services and benefits to which you are otherwise entitled — such as medical insurance coverage for your spouse — are illegal monopoly inducements.

This is just the tip of the iceberg.

In the Presence of God, Pope Francis, and the World:

Let it be known to all living and dead, and to all those responsible for administrating the affairs of the living and dead, that **all commercial contracts** ever actually or presumptively existing between the living man known to the public as **" james-clinton:belcher"** and the living woman known to the public as **"anna-maria:riezinger"** and their similarly named ESTATES and privately held American express and *inter vivos* trusts, including **"Anna M. Riezinger-von Reitz and James C. Belcher"** and the **following incorporated entities** — *the corporate* United States, the city-state of Westminster, United Nations, UNITED NATIONS, the UNITED STATES, Federal Reserve, FEDERAL RESERVE, International Monetary Fund, IMF, and all their respective franchises, agencies, and departments including the State of Alaska and STATE OF ALASKA — **are all and uniformly invalidated** for non-disclosure and semantic deceit.

All signatures of living men and women are rescinded from all documents in the possession of any of these incorporated entities which claim or seek to claim any beneficial commercial interest in them or their ESTATES or which claim any representative capacity related to them or their ESTATES whatsoever.

All interest, good faith service, and accrual on investment owed to the living people as the beneficiaries and entitlement holders of their own ESTATES is due and owed to them and their heirs without exception or prejudice by the officers and administrators of the corporate United States, the city-state of Westminster, and the United Nations.

Be it also known that these and other individual American Nationals now exercise their birthright upon the land of the organic states united by the Articles of Confederation (1781) and that they have the full and unimpeded right to act as Judges of these organic states, to issue orders related to their administration, and to demand compliance with all Articles of the national trust indenture and commercial service contract known as "The Constitution for the united States of America" and all related international treaty provisions owed to us by the corporate United States and the UNITED NATIONS and the city-state of WESTMINSTER, and any successors, executors, administrators, corporate officers, elected or appointed officials, trustees, agents, agencies, franchises, franchise operators, and employees thereof, now and in perpetuity.

To: All Concerned and All Recipients of **FINAL NOTICE** dated **February 3, 2014**

Final Judgment and Civil Orders

Fifty-five (55) days have passed without any sworn affidavit in rebuttal of the facts presented by the FINAL NOTICE OF COMMERCIAL AND ADMINISTRATIVE DEFAULT issued to the individuals, persons, and institutions responsible for default. All have been promptly and properly notified of mis-administration of the public trusts established in the Names/NAMES of living

Americans and the organic American states by incorporated entities doing business as the United States of America, Inc. and the UNITED STATES, INC. and their trustees, officers, employees, and agents who are under contract to provide governmental services to those harmed.

Under the Law of the Sea the claims and demands presented by the FINAL NOTICE OF COMMERCIAL AND ADMINISTRATIVE DEFAULT dated February 7, 2014 are decided and are now in permanent settlement. They stand as **fact** in law.

Notice of the **Motu Proprio** issued by Pope Francis acting as Trustee of the Global Estate Trust on **July 11, 2013**, effective **September 1, 2013**, has been presented to all directly interested parties in Alaska via ancient Edict of Notice: Notice to Principals is Notice to Agents and Notice to Agents is Notice to Principals.

The the corporate United States and the Federal Reserve Banks d.b.a. the United States of America, Inc. and the United Nations City State and its agency the International Monetary Fund, (IMF) d.b.a. UNITED STATES, INC. and its STATE OF ALASKA franchise are commanded and required under contract to the Global Estate Trust to perform according to The Constitution for the united States of America and to cease and desist action against the American people and the organic American states, including Alaskans and the Alaska State created by The Alaska Statehood Compact.

The Alaska Bar Association, its members, the various Court Administrators, and the Alaska Judicial Council have been similarly notified and ordered to cease and desist practices, presumptions, and procedures which serve to defraud living Americans and lay false claims against their private property assets under pretense of war and color of law.

The entities addressed under FINAL NOTICE OF

COMMERCIAL AND ADMINISTRATIVE DEFAULT dated February 7, 2014 are all competent to recognize their culpability and failure to perform under commercial service contract, failure to honor the national and state trust indentures, and failure to provide full and free disclosure of contracts solicited by the named governmental services corporations and agencies cited for default.

Absent a fully disclosed and actual maritime contract entered in evidence and subjected by the court to examination and open discussion, no valid contract can be presumed to exist and no American ESTATE or other vessel can be prosecuted under any maritime or admiralty jurisdiction.

No contract based on unilateral, uninformed, undisclosed, or otherwise prejudicial claims of residency, benefit, status, license, mortgage, or other contract lacking true equitable consideration and consent can be maintained with regard to the ESTATES of American Nationals who are living inhabitants of the Land and Air jurisdictions of the Global Estate Trust, and not naturally subject to the jurisdiction of the Sea.

All such American Nationals who are inhabitants of the land and their ESTATES are additionally protected by treaty and national trust and are owed *safe conduct* for themselves and their commercial vessels on the High Seas and Navigable Inland Waterways. For military tribunal purposes, all American Nationals, American 'persons', and commercial vessels are *non-combatant civilian Third Parties.*

All Provost Marshals, all members of the civilian police forces, all members of the American military, all members of STATE operated National Guard units, all members of government agencies including the U.S. Marshals Service, FBI, State Troopers, BLM, BATF, IRS, and other *code enforcement agents* are ordered to recognize the civil authority of the organic 50 states created by Statehood Compacts and united under The Articles of

Confederation, and to also recognize *the absolute civil authority* of the American people inhabiting these organic and geographically described states in all matters pertaining to them and the administration of their domestic government on the land known as *The United States of America,* not to be confused with *the corporate United States* which is a foreign, maritime entity under commercial contract to provide governmental services for *The United States of America*.

All police and military officers are obligated to honor the **Law of the Land** in all dealings with or pertaining to the organic states and their living inhabitants without exception, noting that these people and states are owed the terms and conditions of the original equity contract known as **The Constitution for the united States of America**, are to be addressed under **American Common Law** exclusively, and that they retain their natural and unalienable rights, including their **natural identity, property rights and controlling interests** without prejudice and regardless of fraud and monopoly inducement practiced against them in breach of trust and contract default.

All actions of the various Probate Courts operating in maritime jurisdictions and merely presuming death based upon the inaction of American National beneficiaries of the American Republic and serving to establish maritime salvage liens against their ESTATES are *by these Orders invalidated*, made null and void. All American Nationals whose names and ESTATES are presently included on tax rolls, and who are recorded by census data, school records, birth certificates, and other public documents **must be presumed to be alive and competent** in the absence of a properly **sworn** Death Certificate signed by the local Coroner stating cause of death, date, time, and place, corroborated by at least two responsible and knowledgeable living witnesses. In the case of legitimately missing people diligent search and fully disclosed publication of all claims against their estates must be made by giving Notice to the last known address and next of kin. Any contrary presumption or practice is fraudulent, null and void.

Any action of the Probate Courts operating in maritime jurisdictions and making claim upon actual real assets of similarly named American Nationals in behalf of legal fiction "missing persons" owned by the corporate United States, the Federal Reserve, or any franchises or agencies thereof, are similarly rendered null and void.

Once created, legal fictions do not have any necessary or valid estate; such estate as they may legitimately be granted must be obtained under conditions of fully revealed and disclosed contract entered into voluntarily and with explicit individual understanding and consent. Any estate obtained by legal fiction entities by process of semantic deceit or undisclosed contract belongs in fact and law to those defrauded. These Civil Orders command and require the return of all titles to land, homes, properties, and businesses which have been held under color of law by the Federal Reserve doing business as the United States of America, Inc., and their bankruptcy Trustee, the Secretary of the Treasury of Puerto Rico, and their administrative agents, including the Custodian of Alien Property and the Comptroller General.

All separate registrations under the Sheppard Towner Act and the Selective Service Act of American Nationals and their progeny by agents of the corporate United States d.b.a. the United States of America, Inc. and its various State franchises and subsequently maintained by STATE franchises of the United Nations and the International Monetary Fund, are invalid as a class for anything but traditional recording purposes and the benefit of any securities based in whole or in part upon these and any other involuntary or undisclosed registrations such as "Vehicle Registrations" are private property benefiting the individual American Nationals who are the lawful entitlement holders of all commercial vessels operated under their given names by any corporation providing governmental services, including banks. All vessels in commerce operated under the names of American Nationals are owed full treaty and trusteeship obligations from the corporate United States and the United Nations and all franchises and agencies which these nation states operate worldwide.

These Civil Orders command performance delivering unto Caesar upon the land, including return of all real assets and property owed to American Nationals free of claim, debt, and encumbrance created under conditions of fraud, breach of trust, and breach of commercial contract.

All judges, attorneys, clerks, and other employees of incorporated courts and court systems, together with the international banks employing them, who have knowingly failed to fully and freely disclose their nature, identity, status, jurisdiction, standing, and venue are subject to international criminal prosecution for felony fraud under full commercial liability and officers of the law and military officers who enforce illegal actions ordered by these in-house international commercial tribunals against American Nationals at the request of any such "court" are responsible for war crimes committed against non-combatant civilians as of September 1, 2013.

All politicians and Trust Management Organization employees acting directly or via franchise or agency who have been elected or appointed to private corporate offices within governmental service corporations, their franchises, or agencies, and who have knowingly pretended to occupy public offices of the American organic states and who have transgressed beyond their limited and private authority are **fully liable** for impersonating American public officials while acting as private corporate officers.

All federal and federal franchise ("State" and "STATE") employees who have **willfully** and **knowingly** conspired to misinform, mislead, mortgage, indebt, extort credit from and otherwise undermine the material interests of American Nationals via non-disclosure, fraud, racketeering, force of arms, extortion, compulsion, semantic deceit and constructive unlawful conversion are guilty of international war crimes against unarmed and non-combatant civilian inhabitants of the land and against commercial vessels belonging by birthright and copyright to those inhabitants.

The United States of America and the city-state of Westminster and its franchises, employees, and agents, are ordered to comply with all stipulations and limitations required by the original equity contract known as "The Constitution for the united States of America" when addressing American Nationals, and when providing any and all government services to American Nationals inhabiting the land of the domestic geographically defined 50 states. They are likewise commanded to release all titles and claims held under color of law against the ESTATES of the American states and the American Nationals inhabiting the organic states of the Union. All incorporated governmental services organizations must immediately cease all action against the material interests of their employers and creditors, the American states and people, and settle all accounts.

There are no so-called "war powers" allowed to any member of Congress representing The United States of America, which has remained at peace since 1865. Likewise, there are no "emergency powers" granted by any of the organic states, no indefinite detainment provisions applicable to any American National under the National Defense Authorization Act 2012 or any similar "Act" of Congress. All "Acts of Congress" undertaken without full commercial liability and not fully enacted as Public Law apply only to the employees and citizens of the corporate United States and no claim of employment or "US citizenship" made by the corporate United States against any inhabitant of the land of the 50 states can be maintained on the basis of undisclosed, unilateral, or second party contract or presumption in violation of the actual American Public Law governing US citizenship, US Statute at Large 2.   •

Any deliberate or systematic use of the given name of any living individual man or woman by **any incorporated entity pretending to represent them or their material interests** to create legal fiction entities operated under-in-or for their name without the full knowledge and consent of that individual is a **prohibited abuse of the rights of usufruct**. All such acts, proposals, programs, and agencies created by the United Nations and by the corporate United States addressed to American Nationals seeking to conscript, obligate, indebt, misinform, or entrap them into any contract whatsoever in which the identity and true nature of the Parties is obscured, not in kind, or wherein the actual terms, claims, conditions, and results of contract are not made explicit, plain, and fully revealed are null and void *ab initio*, as if they never were. All representations serving to misappropriate the good faith and credit of American Nationals and their organic states in favor of any incorporated entity are self-interested, null and void. All registrations, licenses, application processes, and similar devices used by the Federal Reserve d.b.a. United States of America, Inc. and International Monetary Fund d.b.a. UNITED STATES and the FEDERAL RESERVE now operating as an entity incorporated under United Nations auspices, and their various agencies and "state" franchises, are fraudulent, null and void, contrary to Public Law of The United States of America and the individual free states.

Any undeclared agent of <u>the corporate United States</u> or the United Nations caught soliciting such contracts will be arrested, prosecuted, and deported and no further enforcement of such contracts will be allowed on the soil of <u>The United States of America</u> against any birthright inhabitant of the land.

Such foreign, repugnant, and misrepresented commercial contracts include but are not limited to: vehicle registrations, driver licenses, marriage licenses, voter registrations, applications for welfare or medical or

insurance benefits, including "social security insurance", claims of foreign citizenship or foreign personage, residency, mortgages, and public employee retirement benefits.

Parents are not enabled to indebt, pledge, conscript, or otherwise enter their children into any form of bondage, debt, peonage, or enslavement. Any and all relinquishments of individual or parental rights must be voluntary, fully disclosed, completely enumerated, fully discussed, and the real natures and actual identities of all parties to any custodial, commercial, or grant contract of any kind whatsoever, like any agency appointment, must in **all** details be fully revealed and disclosed, explicitly discussed, explicitly agreed upon, and voluntarily entered into by all parties. Any contracts failing these requirements and merely being presumed to exist via tacit agreements, third party representations, or presumed benefit are null and void.

These Civil Orders require that all law enforcement and military officers currently in the employment of The United States of America, the city-state of Westminster, and the United Nations, together with their commercial companies under contract to provide services within the 50 states United be fully and freely informed of these facts and the limitations that are fully applicable to them and their operations on American soil. All American Nationals are to be considered **non-combatant Third Parties** without exception, who are owed peace and protection and performance upon all commercial contracts, treaties, trust indentures, and agreements entered into with the Global Estate Trust and its members, franchises, and agencies.

These Civil Orders also require that corporate administrative tribunals being operated as courts of any kind explicitly and fully declare their identities, natures, venues, services, ownerships, and proper jurisdiction in plain, explicit, fully revealed language with no further purpose of evasion, obstruction, or lack of good faith service. They are additionally commanded to scrupulously observe their limitations and to clearly state their foreign jurisdictions whenever addressing American Nationals.

These Civil Orders come without the corporate United States, without the United Nations, without the city-state of Westminster, without representation, and without prejudice.

NOTICE TO AGENTS IS NOTICE TO PRINCIPALS.
NOTICE TO PRINCIPALS IS NOTICE TO AGENTS.

This Final Judgment and Civil Orders are issued upon our civil, commercial, and canon authority, by our living hands and our testaments jointly sworn and Witnessed by Our Seals and autographs *before Pope Francis and all nations,* declaring that the truth of these matters has been established by due process without rebuttal, and that they have been decided this **11th day of April 2014**. We hereby autograph, seal, and issue this Final Judgment and Civil Orders to all officers, appointees, agents, franchises, agencies, subsidiaries, and employees of the corporate United States, the city-state of Westminster, and the United Nations operating on the land of the 50 organic states of The United States of America and subject them to performance of all treaties and contracts owed as employees, public servants, trustees, administrators, commissioned officers and in all and any capacities whatsoever which allow their presence on our soil and which provide for their strictly defined and limited use of our property:

_____ :

Judge anna-maria-wilhelmina-hanna-sophia:riezinger-von reitzenstein von lettow-vorbeck non-negotiable autograph, under seal and in service, all rights reserved;

_____ :

Judge james-clintwood:belcher non-negotiable autograph under seal and in service, all rights reserved.

5

Answers to Questions

1. What does the Pope, the Holy See, and the Vatican have to do with anything?

All forms of law beginning with Ecclesiastical Law and including the ancient Law Merchant and Law of the Sea, the Roman Civil Law, and most recently, the Uniform Commercial Code and International Criminal Code are ultimately defined by the Holy See and administered by the Roman Curia, under the Trusteeship of the Pope. Control and caretaking of the earlier law forms was undertaken by the Holy See during the First Holy Roman Empire (800 A.D.) and by contract and consent, has remained in the Holy See's control ever since. The two more recent law forms, the Uniform Commercial Code and the International Criminal Code, are copyrighted by Vatican subsidiaries.

The Papacy has functioned in two distinct roles for over 1200 years, exercising both <u>sacred</u> and <u>temporal</u> powers. The Pope is named in two distinct offices and wears two different hats. As the leader of the Church and in sacred office, he is properly regarded as **"<u>His Holiness Pope Francis</u>"**. As the CEO in charge of worldwide commercial affairs executing the temporal powers of the second office, he operates as **"<u>FRANCISCUS</u>"**.

The duties of both offices are distinct and yet ultimately inter-related, due to the Pope's responsibility to oversee **the Global Estate Trust.** Since the 1400's (see Primary Source Reading List) every Pope has acted as the ultimate Trustee and Steward of the entire Earth conceived as a Trust: **the Global Estate Trust.** This Trust, which was created over 400 years ago, is divided into three jurisdictions — **Air, Land, and Sea.** All three are further divided into realms of the **Living** and the **Dead** — the living being actual flesh and blood men and women and animals and other creatures in which the blood flows or sap ascends, the dead being all those organic entities who have died **and all legal fiction entities,** including trusts, corporations, foundations, transmitting utilities, cooperatives, limited liability partnerships and so on.

The **Air Jurisdiction, universal** in chracter, remaining with the Holy See, global, inclusive in nature regardless of individual religious preferences or beliefs, ruling all affairs from the surface of the Earth to the Heavens, is inhabited by spiritual beings both living and dead, has a global population, functions under the Law of Love and the ancient Law of Free Will and is administered via ecclesiastical canon law generally under direction of the Rectors of the National Shrines established in each country.

The **Sea Jurisdiction, international** in character, has an international citizenship, rules all affairs on or directly below the surface of the seas and navigable inland waters, and is inhabited by living men and women known as Merchants and Sailors, and all living sea creatures, as well as all ships and legal fiction entities engaged in maritime and admiralty businesses and contracts, and functions under the Law Merchant (maritime) and Law of the Sea (admiralty) and is administered worldwide by the British Crown Temple d.b.a. Inner City of London a.k.a. "Westminster", and the Lords of the Sea.

The **Land Jurisdiction, national** in character, is inhabited by living men and women, together with land creatures and plants, has a citizenship based on nationality which in most instances includes both the living men and women and legal fiction entities, rules affairs of the land from the surface to the depths beneath, functions under the **Law of the Land** (common law) and is administered worldwide by the Universal Postal Union and the individual national Postmasters.

60

Each jurisdiction — Air, Land, and Sea — has its own law form. The Air functions under ecclesiastical and canon law. The Sea functions under the Law Merchant and Law of the Sea. The land functions under the Law of the Land.

This is the Big Picture, and in the end, it is all administered by the Holy See and the Roman Catholic Church, which has struggled by turns to maintain an "orderly and peaceful Kingdom on Earth" and at times through its history has admittedly been overwhelmed by corruption and human error.

By its nature and function the **Global Estate Trust** has established a vast *interlocking trust directorate* that exists worldwide and extends from the Holy See down to the local level of government administration.

A trust is formed when a **Donor** places assets into the care of a **Trustee** for the good of **Beneficiaries**. In forming the **Global Estate Trust** it was considered that Christ placed the entire planet in the care of St. Peter, that the Pope is Peter's successor Trustee, and over time it has been realized that **all people and living creatures are intended Beneficiaries of the Global Estate Trust**, not just members of the Roman Catholic Church. This realization is one of the most direct results of the **Protestant Reformation,** which asserted **individual dominion over the Earth as granted in Genesis 1:26-28**. Today, as confirmed by Popes John Paul II, Benedict XVI, and Francis, **the Global Estate Trust serves all people regardless of faith, color, or creed.**

2. How does the Global Estate Trust function? Why haven't I heard of it before?

The **Global Estate Trust** is over 400 years old. It was older than The United States of America is today when The United States of America was formed. The **Global Estate Trust** has organized the entire planet according to its system of **postal districts** — also called **"federal districts"** in America. The

Global Estate Trust and the services it provides — legal services, banking services, police services, postal services — is so ubiquitous, so integrated worldwide, that we take its existence for granted and wrongly think that our individual government provides all this.

The truth is that the so-called **"federal government"** in America has always been owned and operated as a private for-profit governmental services company **operating under contract to provide certain designated governmental services,** and — later in history — has been operated as an umbrella corporation with subsidiaries created as franchises and agencies under subcontract to provide these same services by the **Global Estate Trust** and its national subsidiaries.

Side Note: In the eighteenth century when the original **equity contract** known as "The Constitution for the united States" was drawn up, the word **"federal"** was a synonym for **"contract"**, so the nature of the government, as an entity **under contract** to provide services, was apparent to the people. The state legislatures formed to represent the land jurisdiction as separate nations — the larger equivalent of city-states — and the people inhabiting these organic states were clearly aware of the **subservient nature** of the federal government in all matters not clearly delegated to it, as were the Founders and Framers of the Constitution. Article X clearly reserves all other rights to the states and the people.

In summary, our entire planet receives governmental services from one gigantic interlocking trust directorate: the **Global Estate Trust**. The gentleness with which generations of Popes have exercised their power as the ultimate Trustee should not be mistaken for lack of power, but rather as respect for **Free Will** and reluctance to interfere with those entrusted to administer their own affairs. **In the temporal realm a Pope is a man like any other man, and it is often difficult to obtain all the facts and to be assured of right action.** Restraint and tolerance have therefore been the hallmarks governing the exercise of temporal power by the Popes for many decades, but we are now entered upon a time when corruption and criminality have so far progressed among many **governmental service corporations** worldwide that maintaining the role of global trustee has required **action** by the Pope and the Holy See.

Over time, **specialized service centers** organized as separate city-states have taken over specific aspects of the operations of the **Global Estate Trust.** This so-called **"Empire of the City"** spans the globe. Rome and Vatican City remain the home base of operations responsible for overall administration worldwide. **The Inner City of London**, also known as **"Westminster"**, is a separate, independent, international city-state within London and it is home to the **Crown Temple** which administers legal services and is also home to the Fleet Street hub of international banking services. **The District of Columbia**, another city-state, is the center of defense and police services worldwide. **The United Nations**, yet another separate independent city-state, is the hub of international trade, aid, and negotiations.

Over the course of time, delivery of these many services has been organized by separate *for-profit* corporations and organizations operating in each country under the auspices of an umbrella **Trust Management Organization** functioning as the national government. Almost all national governments have been *incorporated* by the Holy See. The American national government is no exception.

The Pope acting in his temporal office, and the Holy See and *its administrative management arms* — the Vatican, the Roman Curia, the British Crown, the Crown Temple, the United Nations, the Pentagon, the Vatican Bank, the Universal Postal Union and a great many other Global Estate Trust franchises and subsidiaries — provide nearly all governmental services worldwide, in addition to their roles administering various *obligations* owed to the many national trusts.

The **Global Estate Trust is by far the largest corporate enterprise on Earth.**

Indeed, the very concept of **"incorporation"** was created by the Holy See and incorporated entities continue to be created and administered entirely under copyrights and administrative law forms of the Roman Curia. The Pope has the undisputed right to liquidate any incorporated entity that is *not functioning lawfully* and according to its charter. He may also order *disposition* of corporate assets to the creditors of any incorporated entity that he liquidates, and can *alter or void* any statute passed by any incorporated government at will.

People don't see the **Global Estate Trust** in the same way that they don't see the Earth beneath their feet. It has always been there. They take it for granted as part of the landscape of the world, but in fact, it is the result of tireless, conscious, determined effort expended over centuries of time. There **is**, in essence, **"one world government"** and it has been here throughout the development of the North American Continent *as a commercial and political power*, from the earliest exploration and colonization down to the present day.

3. What is a "national trust" and why does it matter?

When a new nation is born and enters the international community, **as The United States of America did in 1776**, a contest begins over *representation* of the land and its assets. Once such a contest is resolved, *the Pope,* acting within his temporal office, *as the Donor* of all the assets to be held in the national trust being established, formally recognizes the new nation. As a first step in this process, *a postal district is established and a post office is created for the seat of government*. Benjamin Franklin accomplished this step more than twenty years *before* the American Revolution.

There are *four* very commonly encountered entities that routinely call themselves either *"the United States"* or the *"United States of America"* in some guise, *three "Constitutions"* commonly referred to these entities, and *three versions of "United States Congress"* in play. In all, there are over 350 different legally recognized meanings of the four words *"united states of America"* so it is necessary to draw a line and focus for a moment on only *two* of these entities — those representing actual national trusts.

There is _The United States of America_ that represents the 50 American states acting in perpetual union guaranteed by The Articles of Confederation, and there is _the district United States of America_ that consists of the District of Columbia and "other insular states" — Guam, Puerto Rico, American Samoa, et alia.

To add to the confusion, in addition to these *trust-based entities,* we also have *an incorporated commercial company* doing business as *the United States of America, Inc.,* another commercial company doing business as the **UNITED STATES, INC.**, and additional entities doing business as the **USA**, the **UNITED STATES OF AMERICA**, **E PLURIBUS UNUM THE UNITED STATES OF AMERICA** and so on. Be aware of the semantic confusions and deceits that abound as a result.

Note the slight differences in names — capitalization, punctuation, and prepositions used throughout this document. Each slightly different name or spelling or punctuation denotes a <u>separate</u> legal entity. Boldface is used herein merely to help sort out some of these natural confusions and emphasize important points of interest.

We have **The** US Trust (**major**) and **the** US Trust (**minor**) — both of which are *subsidiary national level trusts* within the **Global Estate Trust**, both operating in tandem in the region of North America. The "states" of the **United States of America (minor)** are "states of America" in the same sense that South American countries are "states of America", e.g., the **Organization of American States** is an organization of what are commonly thought of as **nations**, but which can equally be called **"states"** and also **"American states"** without implying that they are "states" affiliated with **The United States of America (major)** or **the United States of America (minor)**.

When *The US Trust Major* was established to benefit *The United States of America* composed of the now-50 organic states united, the beneficiaries named were *the American people* and their natural and unalienable rights were recognized as assets protected by the national trust indenture contained within the Preamble and Bill of Rights of an *original equity contract* known as *"The Constitution for the united States of America"*.

All inhabitants of **organic, geographically defined states** are living men and women. They are all **owed** *American Common Law* as their law form. The entire civil government **on the land** is vested in each and every single inhabitant. The jurisdiction of the *Air* protects them and their property and interfaces with the governments operating upon *the land jurisdiction* to ensure proper administration.

The governmental services required by the **original Constitution** were provided by a Trust Management Organization operated as a private, for-profit, but **unincorporated company** known simply as **"The United States"**, which was organized by the Founding Fathers, especially Benjamin Franklin, John Adams, Thomas Jefferson, James Madison, Alexander Hamilton, Benedict Arnold, and George Washington

"The Company" known as **"The United States"** was organized in **1754** by Benjamin Franklin. George Washington was its 11th President. As the largest land owner in North America,

Washington was an obvious choice. The foremost *objective* of this *commercial entity*, which was privately fully supported by King George III of England, was the westward expansion of colonization beyond the Appalachian Mountains — in contravention of the **Treaty of the Delawares** which the King had signed with the Native nations just prior to the American Revolution.

From this perspective and from the subsequent *settlements* reached with the leaders of the Revolution, it can be reasonably deduced that the entire operation was conceived, orchestrated, and carried out with the support of European powers merely interested in securing a piece of the much larger pie guaranteed by the westward expansion that was allowed via the artifice of establishing a new government.

Portraits of both *Washington and Franklin* enshrined at the Middle Temple enclave in the Inner City of London suggest that they were in fact *operatives of the Crown* doing King George's dirty work — a fact evident in the Treaty of Paris wherein the King, recognized as *"the Prince" of the United States of America,* is paid tribute in mineral resources, and guaranteed a *perpetual hegemony* governing the commercial and international affairs of all Americans.

Presidents and members of Congress still take their Oath to **"the United States"**, not to the United States **of America** — howbeit, this is a different company called by the same-sounding name — **"the UNITED STATES"**. This gives rise to confusion in the same way that two men called "John" may be mistaken for each other. Watch for this same use of **"mistaken identity"** as an excuse for fraud and despotism throughout the current system.

The Office of President is and always was a private business executive office, not a political one, and as a result, to this day, the President is elected to office by a privately drafted Electoral College, NOT by voters in any General Election.

The original *unincorporated* Trust Management Organization first operated by President George Washington was bankrupted by President Abraham Lincoln on April 24, 1863, as a result of the cost of the Civil War. Eleven years of **"Reconstruction"** — also known as **bankruptcy reorganization** — followed, and a *quiet usurpation* based on semantic deceit, and not-so veiled fraud commenced. The Administration of the American national trust passed on to a **new** Trust Management Organization operated by a **cartel** of international banks (which became the non-federal Federal Reserve) as **"the United States of America"** and doing business as **"the United States of America, Inc."**.

For insight into this, read the **1850 Act of Admissions** which clearly delineates the role and identity of the original organic and unincorporated **"usa"** verses the **United States**, and the difference between the similarly named trust organizations and the commercial service companies. Also read the **Reconstruction Act of 1867 and the Act of 1871** incorporating a **municipal** (city-state) government for the **District of Columbia**.

When the **second** national trust known as "**the US Trust**" was formed to benefit the **new** District of Columbia city-state in 1871, the beneficiaries named were **NOT** "We, the People" of the original national trust, but a mix of living people born in the District of Columbia and other federal enclaves including Puerto Rico; American Negroes who were never granted other citizenship after the Civil War; federal employees; members of the active duty military forces; and **incorporated entities** formed under the auspices of *"the corporate United States"*.

Unlike *The United States of America, the corporate United States* allows corporations organized under its auspices to be **"citizens"**, a fact that has led to no end of fraud and criminality.

All **"US citizens"** have only **"Civil Rights"** — privileges granted by "the **US Congress**". This *separate national entity* initially operated its business affairs as **"United States of America, Inc."** — a corporation chartered in Delaware, under **By-Laws** published as **the Constitution of the United States of America**.

Note the differences in capitalization and the use of the preposition **"of"** in place of **"for"** which distinguishes this version of **"Constitution"** as a *separate legal document* from the original *equity contract* known as **The Constitution for the united States of America**. The agents of *the corporate United States* also popularized **"The Pledge of Allegiance"** as a means of providing *tacit public notice* and securing *assumed consent* for its actions without, however, fully disclosing its nature and intentions or the process of usurpation against *The United States of America* it engaged in.

Please note the *actual words* of The Pledge of Allegiance:

"I (securing a claim of individual consent) **pledge** (an ancient feudal act) **allegiance** (contract) **to the United States of America** (which version is only indicated by the lack of capitalization on the word "the") **and to the Republic** (the original organic states' government) **for which it stands, one nation, under God, indivisible, with liberty and justice for all."**

Note that there hasn't been "one nation" since 1871. There have been *two nations* operating under *two separate* administrative protocols and *two national trusts,* but it has been the subversive objective of Congress to join both into one entity and *operate it as an oligarchy,* just as the Congress currently operates *the corporate United States* as an oligarchy.

The Pledge of Allegiance — an innocuous-appearing mantra endlessly repeated in public schools and public meetings across America is a **VERBAL CONTRACT** secretly obligating the victims to accept representation of their Republic by **"the United**

States of America" which failed to properly identify itself or seek open consent, and which merely *claimed* to "stand for" the American Republic.

The Pledge of Allegiance is an undisclosed **entrapment into unlawful contract** ceding authority to represent the individual inhabitants and the American Republic to **"the United States of America"** similar to what happens when an unwary individual hires a lawyer to **"re-present"** him and **"stand for"** him in a court. **The representative gains a largely unaccountable controlling interest in the affairs of his actual employer who is relegated to the status of an incompetent ward of the state, or a state dependent.**

As a result of this semantic duplicity and deceit, no valid *new* contract between *the organic American states* and *the corporate United States* was ever established. The "Constitution **of** the United States of America" remains a document peculiar to *the corporate United States*, not to be confused with the original equity contract known as **"The** Constitution **for** the united States of America".

At the beginning of last century there were two completely separate versions of "United States of America" operating, and two kinds of "US (C)itzens" and two "Constitutions" and the "US Congress" was acting in *two roles* in conflict of interest. The original Constitution known as **"The** Constitution **for** the united States of America" and the By-Laws of the newly formed federal corporation known as **"the** Constitution **of** the United States of America" formed under the auspices of *the corporate United States*.

All this <u>semantic deceit</u> was and is extremely complex and is deliberately designed to defraud and confuse.

A separation of the Land jurisdiction and Sea jurisdiction was set up from the very founding of **The** United States of America and made part of the Treaty of Paris; the Treaty of Westminster (with the Inner City of London: a separate international City-State); and the Treaty of Ghent, et alia, however, it was never envisioned that the District of Columbia would form a **separate** city-state and operate a **separate national government under deceptively similar names**, by allowing members of Congress to wear **two hats** creating **two kinds** of "citizenship".

These two separate national trusts operated under deceptively similar names have co-existed for almost 150 years, but the semantic deceit involved has resulted in endless confusion, fraud, breach of trust, and ultimately in the *identity theft* practiced by *the corporate United States* against *The United States of America*.

Additional insight into this development of "two Americas" can be gained by reading the **Insular Tariff Cases** (1900-1904) — the most famous of which is *Downes v. Bidwell*.

The separate National Trusts create two separate nations— **The** United States of America which includes the 50 domestic States bound in perpetual union by The Articles of Confederation (1781) and **the** United States of America (*the corporate United States*) which represents the District of Columbia (formally renamed the "State of New Columbia" in 1984) in union with the so-called "Insular States" comprised of "federal possessions and territories". The circumstance also created two kinds of citizen — U.S. **C**itizens and US **c**itizens as already noted.

The United States of America (**major**) is a Republic composed geographically defined states and inhabited by living men and women. These states (small "**s**") are all formed by Statehood Compacts. This version of United States of America functions under the **Law of the Land** which is **the American Common Law** and the federal government — that is the Trust Management Organization charged with protecting **The** U.S. Trust and providing the nineteen stipulated governmental services under contract — is restricted by The Constitution for the united States of America.

Members of "The United States of America in Congress assembled" are obligated to function under complete commercial liability and as a sovereign Body Politic, with the result that no "Congress" has occupied these offices since 1865, and with the further result that no substantive and fully enacted **Public Law** affecting **U.S. Citizens** has been passed since then. The organic states and the people inhabiting them have been silent since December of 1865, a circumstance that unscrupulous individuals have used as an excuse to claim that the American government is defunct — despite the fact that the actual civil government is embodied in each and every living American.

As you will note upon reading the Admissions Act of 1850, the Congress operating as a Body Politic is the **"congress of the united states of america"** operating as the **"senate"** and the **"house of representatives"** directly representing the living American People and the Republic states. When operating as the **true representative government** of The United States of America (**major**) the names of these political bodies are NEVER capitalized. This is not a typographical error or the result of quaint old language conventions. This is part of the *language of law* that has existed since Roman times.

The United States of America (**minor**) is a Commonwealth inhabited by **"US citizens"** — a **mix** of living people and incorporated entities. This separate city-state is operated as an oligarchy by the members of the **"US Congress"**. It functions entirely under the law forms of international commerce (maritime) and Admiralty. The **"US Congress"** of the United States of America (**minor**) also operates as the Board of Trustees of the United States of America, Inc., and its members enjoy limited liability — with the result that they can only pass **"Public Policy"**, not Public Law. Increasingly, this out-of-control oligarchy has functioned in a criminal, despotic, irresponsible, and reckless manner, disrespecting its contractual obligations to The United States of America (major), misrepresenting itself "as" The United States of America (major), and facilitating numerous kinds of fraud, racketeering, and inland piracy against the American People inhabiting the 50 States, while pursing increasingly violent and criminal activities overseas — trading in drugs, prostitution, alcohol, arms, and other "federally controlled" substances.

The national trusts — which are all donated by the Pope in his capacity as the **Global Estate Trustee** — are important because they define the assets of the nation and the beneficiaries of the trust. **They also obligate specific parties to act as Trustees and to protect the nation under trust indenture and contract.**

The Pope is the Ultimate Trustee and the Global Trustee of the Air Jurisdiction. The Rector of the National Shrine is responsible for administration of this jurisdiction in the United States of America (minor), and is therefore responsible for holding their administrators accountable.

The British Monarch is our Trustee on the High Seas and Inland Waterways and is directly accountable for protecting us and our commercial "vessels" in the international jurisdiction where our rights and material interests have been violated.

The U.S. Postmaster is our Trustee on the Land, but owing to the corruption of the government already described, that office was vacated and released. In correction, Pope Benedict XVI established a new Postmaster Office to provide oversight for all of North America in 2010.

4. <u>You've charged that there is commercial and administrative default — why? What is this bankruptcy you keep talking about?</u>

There are actually several bankruptcies involved, beginning with the bankruptcy of **The United States (Company)** in April of **1863**. That resulted in Abraham Lincoln creating the Lieber Code, also known as General Order 100, and making the U.S. Army responsible for safeguarding the nation's money. **The United States of America (major)** still operates under the Lieber Code and despite no less than three (3) public declarations ending the Civil War by President Andrew Johnson, **the U.S. Army continues to control and administer the government of the Republic.** This is how we get offices containing military titles like Inspector **General**, **Lieutenant** Governor, and US Postmaster **General**.

This is also why we have been kept **in a constant state of "war"** — at least on paper — since 1860. Over time, public knowledge of the circumstance and the Lieber Code has faded, leaving the U.S. Army to increasingly function without any oversight or restraint. The Understanding of their role as guardians of the Republic and the people has also faded within the ranks, **until today we are faced with the possibility of having the President of a foreign commercial corporation ordering our own troops to fire on us.** We may all thank God that the Holy See remembers things long after others forget, and has the resources to remind the U.S. Army of its real purpose and mission.

Next, there was the bankruptcy of the United States of America, **Inc.,** in **1933**, by Executive Order of its President, Franklin Delano Roosevelt. The Creditors of this commercial bankruptcy — the World Bank, The International Bank for Reconstruction and Development (IBRD), and The non-federal Federal Reserve (the IMF claims to represent **all** creditors including the living Americans who were named the **priority creditors**) — appointed the **Secretary of the Treasury of Puerto Rico** to act as the US Bankruptcy Trustee.

Yet still to come is the bankruptcy of the CORPORATE

UNITED STATES, a French commercial corporation named after the original "United States" which was bankrupted in 1863, and formed to administer the *governmental services contracts* of the United States of America, Inc., during its bankruptcy reorganization.

These bankruptcies of the Trust Management Organizations providing governmental services to Americans have **all been planned** — to provide vast profit for the perpetrators, and equally great losses to the American people.

The Great Bankruptcy Fraud
This is the essence of the bankruptcy fraud:

One Trust Management Organization (incorporated) creates "franchises" named after individual living Americans; runs up huge bills against these **legal fiction entities,** and leaves the hapless living people of "similar name" to pay the bills, or have their credit wrecked and their private property assets seized — while skipping off and filing for bankruptcy protection for itself.

Meanwhile, a *second* incorporated Trust Management Organization sets up shop under a similar name and takes over the service contracts "in behalf of" the former TMO undergoing bankruptcy reorganization; creates its own set of franchises named after living Americans, and runs up huge bills against these separate legal fiction entities leaving the hapless living people of similar name to pay the bills or have their credit wrecked and their private property assets seized — while also skipping off and filing for bankruptcy protection for itself.

Repeat this TMO action as necessary — for as long as you can get away with it.

The two Trust Management Organizations currently involved are both operated by international banking cartels. The none-federal Federal Reserve, which is as "federal" as Federal Express, operates the United States of America, Inc. The United Nations, Inc. doing business as the International Monetary Fund, Inc. (IMF) operates the "secondary" front organization doing business as the UNITED STATES, INC.

As of **July 1, 2013**, the hapless American people mistaken as sureties and their Estates functioning under names in the form "John Quincy Adams" — paid off all the debts, all the interest, all the trumped up service charges that were brought against them as a result of the bankruptcy of the United States of America, Inc., in 1933. The United States of America, Inc. was **released** from bankruptcy and all its debts were settled as of that date.

The Federal Reserve has meanwhile re-named and re-invented itself as a **new** corporation organized under the auspices of the United Nations, a separate city-state, and is doing business internationally as the **FEDERAL RESERVE**. Meaning, it is no longer an American institution and is operating under UN charter and rules.

At the same time, the UNITED STATES, INC. is running up trillions of dollars of debt against the credit of its own brand of manufactured-out-of-thin-air "sureties" — Puerto Rican ESTATE trusts operated under the NAMES of living Americans in the form "JOHN QUINCY ADAMS" — with the clear intention of having Barack Obama declare bankruptcy just as FDR declared bankruptcy — leaving the hapless living Americans of "similar name" to pay off the trumped up debts of the UNITED STATES, INC., while it seeks bankruptcy protection, in turn.

The newly organized "FEDERAL RESERVE" (major) is busily populating America with yet another new set of "franchises" — these *new* legal fiction entities named after living Americans are all being named in this form: "JOHN Q. ADAMS", which isn't even a legal, identifiable name, and they are all transmitting utilities.

When people pay bills addressed to these *new* entities and appear to "accept" these new names — having been misled into assuming that these entities are the same as the living people — the charlatans will have *carte blanch* to make a whole new con game set up for themselves, assert *new* claims against the people and the states "redefined" as public transmitting utilities, and not be bound by "specificity".

Please note that "JOHN Q. PUBLIC" could be "JOHN QUINCY PUBLIC" or "JOHN QUENTIN PUBLIC" or, or, or... The lawyers among us know perfectly well that "JOHN Q. PUBLIC" is not a legal name. It is purely a commercial, trademarked name belonging to a corporation as chattel, and the reason this change is being attempted is that the IMF is no longer able to charge off the cost of providing government services to the ESTATES of the American People which were improperly held as "sureties" backing the debts of the United States of America, Inc. — a "doing business name" of the old Federal Reserve System.

It is imperative that this scheme be recognized and stopped at the onset and that these false claims by the none-federal FEDERAL RESERVE be objected to immediately, individually, and collectively.

Their intention is clear and its history is cast in cement. These Trust Management Organizations have committed gross breach of trust, gross fiduciary malfeasance, gross unlawful conversion, gross identity theft, gross conspiracy to defraud. They are international crime syndicates in every sense of those words, and they are on the verge of repeating their past history. Like parasites, they have simply "moved on" to other hosts, passing from The United States of America (major) to the United States of America (minor) and now to the United Nations City-State.

The federal reserve, an **unincorporated** association of banks operating under the auspices of **The United States of America** (**major**) in 1900, moved on to become the **Federal Reserve**, an **incorporated** association of banks operating under **the United States of America (minor) circa 1930**, and it is now moving on, again, to function as the **FEDERAL RESERVE**, an entity incorporated under the auspices of the **United Nations**, which is a separate, independent, **international city-state** that has allowed the FEDERAL RESERVE to be incorporated under its auspices.

The Pope, in issuing the ***Motu Proprio*** of July 11, 2013, has said in effect — "**Enough!** You are liable and will be held liable as of September 1, 2013."

This continued identity theft and pillaging of private property "in the name of public trusts" is no longer going to be allowed. The resources of the entire **Global Estate Trust** will be mobilized to make sure that this pattern of abuse does not continue. Each and every one of you addressed has participated knowingly or unknowingly in some capacity necessary to the success of this gargantuan fraud and you are now being notified of the facts and encouraged to self-correct, or pay the piper.

It would not be right or fair to sweep up the innocent with the guilty, so you have **all** been given multiple notices and opportunities to learn the facts. The Trust Management Organizations themselves have been given three (3) years in which to correct their operations from top to bottom or face dissolution of their charters and disposition of their assets. From the perspective of the **Global Estate Trust**, it doesn't matter where the 'federal reserve' banks run and hide or under which national entity they choose to incorporate. The basic issues remain the same and everyone on earth has a stake in bringing this system of fraud and enslavement to an end. Everyone who works for or under the auspices of the Roman Curia — everyone in the legal profession from the lowliest clerks to the highest judges — became **100% liable** for their acts and omissions with regard to these issues as of September 1, 2013.

All this is why we have brought **FINAL NOTICE OF COMMERCIAL AND ADMINISTRATIVE DEFAULT**, and this is why we keep talking about bankruptcies. Unless everyone recognizes his own culpability and takes action accordingly **to pre-empt it**, there will be another manufactured "national" bankruptcy in the near future and billions of people worldwide will suffer, to the profit of a few hundred masterminds at the top of the pyramid scheme.

5. How is *our* money involved?

A partial answer was provided above. When the Trust Management Organization doing business as the UNITED STATES declares bankruptcy the living people will again be **"presumed"** to be sureties for its debts — absent concerted effort to derail the cycle of engineered national bankruptcies. Those international investors who are owed money by the UNITED STATES, INC. will come knocking on the doors of millions of Americans, under the false presumption that these people agreed to stand as sureties for the debts of Harry Reid, Nancy Pelosi, et alia, all doing business as the UNITED STATES, INC.

This is constructive fraud based on semantic deceit and identity theft being carried out by private, for-profit, largely foreign corporations operating on American soil under charters and treaty arrangements that they have abundantly and criminally violated.

Your **currency** — not your "money" — is inevitably involved, because for eighty years you have been passing around paper I.O.U's instead of any form of money. A "note" is an I.O.U. and a "Federal Reserve Note" (FRN) is an I.O.U. from the Federal Reserve Banks. **It is impossible to pay a debt with an I.O.U. You can only go deeper into debt as a result of this practice.** A negative, plus a negative, **never** equals a positive.

Here is the circumstance: you owe $500 and you have no actual money to pay this debt. The only "legal tender" in circulation is in the form of I.O.U. Notes issued by the Federal Reserve Banks. Joe Average American — deliberately placed in this situation by the perpetrators of this fraud — is under **monopoly inducement** and has no choice but to "pay" his debts with I.O.U.'s, and thereby **become a debtor** instead of becoming a creditor.

If I give you an I.O.U. as payment of a debt, I have not paid my debt. I have only postponed payment of my debt to a later time. That's what the Federal Reserve has done — collected debt upon debt upon debt and never paid a dime toward any of it, since 1933.

What happens when you go out and earn $500.00 worth of Federal Reserve Notes? Your labor allows you to pass off the debt to the Federal Reserve. You are out of the frying pan for the moment, but **the debt is still unpaid**. That's how the "National Debt" accumulates exponentially. In such a system, nobody ever gets paid for anything — the debt just gets passed around and builds up and up and up no matter how hard you work or how productive you may be. And **interest** is accuring on that debt.

Instead of being what you actually are, a nation of creditors, you are reduced by sleight of hand and fraud and monopoly inducement to being debtors by definition, and you can never get out of the cycle of false "debt" until you recognize the fraud for what it is, and stop playing the game, and put an end to it.

What does the Federal Reserve do with all this debt it has been collecting for eighty years? It enters it as a credit for itself against your estate. Not only has your original debt not been paid, but interest and service fees have been added to it, and that has all accumulated against your estate —against your body, your labor, your home, your business, your copyrights and intellectual property.

What happened to the value of your original labor that you expended to earn Federal Reserve Notes? **It never gets credited to you.** It is siphoned off by the same people who bring you this incredible fraud. Your credit is being kept in "off book accounts" belonging to YOUR NAME — a Puerto Rican Estate trust — and after a period of time, the banks claim these assets as "abandoned funds". They are holding the entire National Debt against the estates of living Americans and pretending that you and your parents and grandparents did nothing but sit on your rumps since 1933.

Every American who ever signed up for Social Security — having first been blatantly lied to and coerced by undeclared Foreign Agents of the corporate United States and told that Social Security was a retirement insurance program and that it was a mandatory requirement of having a job in America — is claimed to be an **unpaid volunteer employee** of the "federal government" corporation by the perpetrators of this con game and therefore is a "US citizen" instead of an American National.

Unknown to those same American Nationals, the corporations masquerading as their lawful government use their "voluntary application" for "Social Security benefits" to obtain a veiled general Power of Attorney hidden in the SS-5 Form, and seize control of their ESTATES. They then set up two accounts "in their names"; one administered by the **"IRS"** for the **Federal Reserve** and the other one administered by the **"IRS"** for the **International Monetary Fund.** One account is set up as the **debt side** account following the familiar pattern: **123-45-6789**. The other account is set up as the **credit side** account using the same numbers without hyphens: **123456789**.

Most American Nationals are owed several million dollars worth of credit owed to their individual ESTATE accounts, but the perpetrators of the fraud never disclose this fact. The "richest people on earth" live as debt slaves to international banking cartels that have obtained this position by fraud.

The final cherry on top is that these same banking interests use your tax money to buy million dollar life insurance policies on each and every "US citizen" — benefiting the bank of course — when the citizen passes on. Thus, the banks contrive to profit from you even at the end of your lives, and they always have a profit motive to have you killed. Killing off young people through war brings more profit, which, together with stealing natural resources to manipulate commodity markets, explains why promoting *wars for profit* are favorite pastimes for these unspeakably corrupt and evil corporate entities.

The same situation applies in Canada, Australia, New Zealand, and most of Europe. The same nine digit accounting system is used throughout, and abused in the same ways worldwide.

6. <u>What is convertible debt?</u>

A **convertible debt is any form of debt that can be converted into another form of debt.** Federal Reserve Notes can be converted into mortgages, stocks, bonds, annuities — any other "debt instrument" or "debt based security". **A fraudulent convertible debt is a debt that is created by fraud and then converted.** That's what we have going on in America today.

Pull up the Bankruptcy Act and look at Section 101(11). There you will see who the actual Creditors of the Trust Management Company, that FDR bankrupted in 1933, are — the living people. Americans at that time, and their heirs, were the Priority Creditors and Entitlement Holders, but because of the *monopoly inducement* explained in Item 5, you've been arbitrarily "redefined" as "debtors" instead.

What happens when you pay an electric bill addressed to the federal franchise ESTATE trust currently doing business under your NAME as a franchise of the UNITED STATES, INC.? You become a debtor instead of a creditor so long as you pay it in Federal Reserve Notes. The utility company seizes these debt notes, you've so graciously provided to them for free, and converts them into other forms of debt — buying up stocks, bonds, insurance policies, etc. — benefiting itself.

The "debt" thus created is fraudulent on three counts — **first**, it is the by-product of illegal *monopoly inducement* forcing you to use Federal Reserve Notes as legal tender; **second**, it is a debt owed by the federal franchise ESTATE trust doing business "in your name" but deceitfully presented to you as if it were your debt; and **third**, you have been coerced to pay a billing **"statement"** instead of a **real bill**.

So we have a debt created by fraud converted into other forms of debt benefiting — in this example — a utility company which reinvests "your" Federal Reserve Notes in other forms of debt. That is fraudulent convertible debt in practice.

This is yet another way in which you are being defrauded and the value of your labor and other resources is being converted to benefit incorporated entities at the expense of you and your private estate.

Next time you get a tax bill, a utility bill, a credit card bill or any other "bill" addressed to YOUR NAME IN ALL CAPITAL LETTERS, look at it very closely with the understanding that **(1)** the item is addressed to a Puerto Rican "federal franchise" ESTATE trust doing business in your NAME, not to you; **(2)** the item is a "billing statement" or "billing summary" or some other name, but never an actual Bill, so technically even the ESTATE has not been billed; **(3)** these billing statements are not denominated in dollars — except occasionally by mistake — the "amount owed" appears as a series of numbers, commas, and dots similar to that used to write dollar amounts, but there is no dollar sign and no words indicating the kind or form of money or currency that is supposedly owed.

For example, your property tax bill will show up addressed to YOUR NAME and the statement will show that YOUR NAME owes a number written like this: 6,955.43 for 2013 or that YOUR NAME'S house has a value of: 258,990.00 according to the Tax Assessor's Office. **These are just deceptively constructed series of numbers, dots, and commas designed to make you assume that these represent dollar amounts.** Again, technically, not even the ESTATE has been billed for anything.

It's all *constructive fraud* based on semantic deceit, illusion, and processes of assumption knowingly pursued under conditions of non-disclosure.

This is done on purpose, with malice aforethought. The perpetrators are giving you notice that a bill *related to the ESTATE named after you* **exists**, but they are actually and purposefully preventing you from paying it. If they sent a **real Bill**, you could either discharge it through the U.S. Treasury Window at any Federal Reserve Bank, or, you could present it for payment under UNCITRAL and exchange it against your Birth Certificate Bond or other assets held by the US Bankruptcy Trustees in your name. This process of discharging debts, unlike using Federal Reserve Notes, **actually pays the bill**, and since the entire game is about forcing you to *indebt yourself*, the perpetrators spare no effort to prevent you from discharging the bills related to *their* "federal" ESTATE trust.

Another reason they refuse to provide you with an actual Bill is because what they are doing is a crime.

As long as they are sending these "billing statements" to a federal franchise ESTATE trust, they technically can't be accused of billing **you**. As long as they don't provide you with an actual Bill, they can't be accused of false billing, either. According to them, they don't know what you are talking about. What bill? We never sent that man a bill… we sent a **billing statement** addressed to a **Puerto Rican ESTATE trust** that "just happens" to have the same name and address. Who cares if we fully intend to force and coerce the living man to pay us with an I.O.U. and owe us even more debt after he "paid" than when he started?

7. <u>Are you telling me that I don't owe any taxes? How is that possible? It costs money to provide governmental services. If I don't pay my taxes, how will the schools be funded and the fire departments and libraries stay open?</u>

The fact is that **all** governmental services contracts are between states and other incorporated entities, not between states and people. **Technically, it's literally *impossible* for a living man or woman to owe any tax for any governmental service.**

Remember that all valid contracts must be "in-kind". Corporations can only contract with other corporations. Living people can only contract with other living people. The proliferation of "trusts" has been used as a vehicle — literally creating a "commercial vessel" capable of interfacing with corporations and entering into corporate contracts. The creation of these "individual public trusts" and their supposed obligations has been done **without** the knowledge, consent, or participation of the living people, merely upon the "representations" made "in their behalf" by third parties claiming to "represent" them — lawyers and unscrupulous politicians.

Note that even the original equity contract known as The Constitution for the united States of America is between the States and the government being created by contract to provide the States with services — not the living people. We, the People, are only mentioned as the **beneficiaries** of the Natural and Unalienable Rights that are assets held in the national trust and further outlined and defined by the Bill of Rights. **We are not direct parties to this or any other governmental services contract.**

As for, how do governmental services get paid for? Your states are inestimably valuable, and properly administered, they contain vast material assets that can be utilized to generate income more than sufficient to pay for all governmental services — and this is in fact what **all** the states do. **They *already* generate more than enough income every year to pay for all governmental services.** They simply keep track of their expenses and provide a "billing statement" addressed to your ESTATE in hopes that you will step forward and "volunteer" — to pay a share of the expenses **for them**, so that their private, for-profit corporation is enabled to operate without any expense, and seize the entire profit from the sale, utilization and investment of your organic state's assets, entirely for its own benefit.

If by chance your ESTATE fails to voluntarily cough up its share this year, they will conveniently forget all the other labor and currency and value you have contributed in prior years, and also fail to mention all the money they made this year off of the "state" assets that **you** are supposed to be the beneficiary of. Alaskans should at this point take a moment to estimate their actual share of revenue collected from the oil industry this year, versus the pittance offered as a "Permanent Fund Dividend". Now, they should calculate their actual share of the Permanent Fund Dividend, as shareholders. And they should, if they are rational beings, be very, very upset with those claiming to "represent" them, and their interests.

After all, those who claim to "represent" you have taken seats as the officers of this same foreign franchise for-profit "STATE" corporation and they see it as their duty to make sure that that corporation is as profitable as possible — so they justify attacking you, their employer, and seizing your assets and telling you what to do and how to do it and when and how often — all in the name of somehow ultimately benefiting you via entrapment, enslavement, armed extortion, and fraud.

86

Every unit of "government" in America is not only in control of, and profiting from, the use and misuse of vast "public" assets, they are rolling in the money and credit they have extorted from the actual beneficiaries of the public trusts, then rolling in some more in the money and credit they have made from investing all this purloined largesse, and proliferating new and ever-more numerous units of government and government agencies — like a cancerous growth soaking up the sugars of the Body Politic.

Every year the corporations running your federal, state, and municipal "government" make so much more money than they expend on public services, that the idea that taxation of individual living men and women and their private property assets is "necessary" to fund public services, is laughable. Exactly how these criminally mismanaged corporations hide the loot so that they can continue to "poor mouth" and impose more taxation, will be addressed in answer to other questions.

8. Why are the courts at fault?

In 1938 following a Supreme Court case known as *Erie Railroad v. Thompkins,* executives from the Roosevelt Administration called a meeting with the US Supreme Court Justices; Senior Judges from all the Circuit and Appellate Courts; and the most prominent lawyers of the times; and they told them a purposeful self-interested lie. The executives said that the United States of America was bankrupt — they just neglected to say *which* "United States of America" *and what form of* "United States of America" they were talking about. The executives also told the legal professionals that because of this bankruptcy, they were to operate their courts ONLY in maritime jurisdictions. Verbatim: *"We don't care what you call it, but only operate maritime and admiralty courts.*

From that time to this, this is what the members of the American Bar Association have done. They have run a fantastic gamut of "courts" pretending to operate as "state courts" and "custody courts" and "US DISTRICT COURTS" and "Superior Courts" and on and on — pretending to operate courts at equity and under civil law, but the entire time they have operated exclusively as maritime courts and as in-house corporate tribunals.

The courts are at fault because they know that they are routinely operating in jurisdictions that have nothing to do with the cases before them.

The courts are at fault because they know they are operating in maritime jurisdictions and pretending otherwise. They are at fault because they have accepted ***unilateral contracts*** as "valid" maritime contracts. They are at fault because they do not require proof of any ***valid maritime jurisdiction,*** even when called on the carpet for failure to do so. The list goes on.

Why have the courts malfunctioned in this way and continued on this course for almost eighty years? Part of it is ignorance. A great many American jurists have grown up under these conditions and they don't know that anything different ever existed. Many don't know that **"statutory law" is maritime law** and if the judges and lawyers don't know, who does? Some don't even know that "statutory law" applies uniquely to statutory entities — legal fictions created by statute.

The rest of the reason is pure corruption and graft for profit on the part of those who ***do*** know what is going on.

"Federal" judges have issued standing orders to "invest" all court cases through the Court Registry Investment System (CRIS) — that is, to "deposit" all cases **as securities** into the Dallas Texas Federal Researve Bank.

Every such court case is assigned a US Treasury Public Debt Number — a Docket Number in "State" courts, and a Case Number in "US DISTRICT COURTS". This makes every court case a "securituzed" financial transaction.

After the Public Debt Number is issued, which converts the court case into a counterfeit obligation under 18 USC 472, et seq. 473, 474; the Court Administrator counterfeits the same debt obligation again by adding a CUSIP number to the "Instrument". One counterfeit obligation benefits the Federal Reserve, the other one benefits the IMF.

CUSIP is an acronym for Committee on Uniform Securities Identification Procedures. CUSIP is a copyrighted and registered trademark of The American Bankers Association (ABA). The court administrators work for the banks, not any "court system" unless you want to call it the Court Bank, where the bank always wins.

At this point in the fraud, the "court administrator" working for the banks has converted every court case into a banking financial securities instrument — which puts the court itself into the position of being "creditor" and **both** the plaintiff and the defendant are cast into the role of "debtors".

The judges are acting with a vested interest with insider knowledge and they are insider trading in complete and utter violation of the judicial canons.

They cannot act without bias when the quantity and quality of their salaries, benefits, and retirement packages are sitting in the docket every day awaiting their "investment". Rather than ruling on the merits, arguments, or even the facts, they are making financial investments in every case — futures contracts, in a future they can direct.

They are running a rigged gambling operation out of the courthouse, under the noses of the Alaska State Troopers, the FBI, and the US Marshals, who all turn to these icons of rectitude for "legal" advice instead of using their own noses and common sense to determine what is lawful.

The judges and court administrators are also committing tax fraud by shifting the "debt" created by every case onto the individual(s) who are actually the Creditor(s) in every case, and converting the case into an investment security belonging to the Dallas Federal Reserve Bank instead, which in turn shifts the money from the Creditor side of the "transaction" into the pockets of the Debtors. **They are deceptively laundering a fraudulent debt into corporate assets belonging to the bank, and converting those assets into revenue sharing funneled back to the Department of Transportation (Federal Reserve) or DEPARTMENT OF TRANSPORTATION (IMF) franchises, respectively.**

So in addition to running a rigged gambling operation out of the courthouses, the courts are also laundering vast amounts of fraudulently procured credit assets back into the operations side of the two colluding Trust Management Organizations. A whopping percentage of the total take from all this securities fraud goes into the judge's retirement fund also administered by the Dallas Federal Reserve Bank.

It is self-explanatory why the courts and their administrators are at fault for this entire situation, that it is outrageous and not to be tolerated, and also why it must come to a halt and be brought to a halt by those responsible for administration of these entities. Any jurist who values his or her "law license" issued by an international banking cartel being operated as a criminal syndicate more than he or she values the law deserves to be disbarred — and will be.

9. In one of the demonstration cases you repeatedly made a great issue of whether or not the Judge was acting as a trustee or not, and at one point even offered to appoint him directly as your trustee. Why?

I did this to determine and place on the record which "hat"

he was wearing. According to Section 3 of Article XIV of the Constitution of the United States of America — the Federal Reserve corporation d.b.a. United States of America, Inc., By-Laws — all public employees are trustees.

The question of trusteeship is vital. Public employees under both "The Constituton for the united States of America" and "the Constitution of the United States of America" and all the related subsidiary "State Constitutions" are openly declared and required to act as trustees to protect the respective National Trusts. It has been the erroneous practice of the UNITED STATES, INC., and its STATE franchises to forget about their obligations in this respect, and to concentrate entirely on the juicy federal services contracts they inherited during the bankruptcy reorganization of the United States of America, Inc.

The "Constitution of the United States" (yet another separate Constitution) under which the UNITED STATES, INC., was organized has no mention of trusteeship, but that doesn't mean the fiduciary obligations vanished simply because a successor Trust Management Organization has tried to ignore them. It only means that judges who don't admit to being trustees are **admittedly** operating in the foreign international jurisdiction of the IMF organization.

This was already implied by the title block style of the header on the case, but settling the Trustee matter forced the JUDGE to give up any pretension of *in personam* jurisdiction and to reveal the actual venue of the proceedings, which he otherwise attempted to obscure.

Throughout that case the JUDGE took an active litigant's stance and practiced law — liberally — from the bench, flagrantly acting in support of the bank's attorney. Several times during the proceedings the Judge was observed smiling, winking, and nodding to her. Although we entered Special Appearance throughout and demanded proof of jurisdiction from the outset — and even though the bank's attorney is required to prove jurisdiction beyond reasonable doubt by canon law — she made no attempt to do so beyond a naked verbal assertion that the ESTATES "resided in Alaska" — which has no meaning in a verbal context, because it is impossible to determine which version of "Alaska" is being referenced.

During the first Hearing, the JUDGE deliberately obscured the venue and jurisdiction of the court, claiming that his authority derived from "the de jure Constitution of the State of Alaska" — a document that doesn't exist, **which would obligate him to act as our trustee** if it did. Soon after making this claim, the JUDGE made an excuse to leave the courtroom and formally changed the jurisdiction of the proceedings under the pretense of getting copies of a document for us. This only served to move the in-house corporate tribunal to Special Admiralty. Nobody operating under judicial canon would engage in such deceitful behavior, nor would anyone operating an honest court have reason to engage in such arcane procedure.

By process of elimination, it stands that THE SUPERIOR DISTRICT COURT FOR THE STATE OF ALASKA, INC. was operating an agency-based *"federal" debt collection procedure process* against privately owned and operated international *inter vivos* trusts under the presumption that they were instead ESTATE franchises of the UNITED STATES, INC., operated in arrears by federal employees. This was all set up and maintained in the face of open and un-rebutted objection, without jurisdiction, in the absence of any validated claim or authority, whatsoever, to address us, the living principals, beneficiaries of the ESTATES, and Priority Creditors.

Part of the corruption of the courts is that they do not openly, freely, and honestly reveal the jurisdiction they are operating in at any given time, and do not discuss the presumptions — often far-fetched presumptions — that they are operating under. In the demonstration case, 3AN-12-6858CI, the JUDGE claimed to be operating the court under the administrative auspices of the United States of America (minor)'s local franchise, the State of Alaska, then used a subterfuge to change that declared jurisdiction to international maritime jurisdiction without disclosure. This sort of "bait and switch" artifice is inherently fraudulent and leads inevitably to self-interested and purposeful confusion at law.

10. Who are you? How do you know all this?

Our families have struggled with the administration of the Holy Roman Empire — and the **Global Estate Trust** — in all its guises, for over a thousand years. There is no lie that a banker can utter that we haven't heard a dozen times before. There is no scam that a con artist can conceive that we haven't already dealt with.

Now, it's your turn.

We are tired of reading the entire list of Primary Source Documents and reference books included for your interest, plus hundreds more arcane documents detailing the attempts of Popes and Kings and Presidents and Congresses to do things both wonderful and horrible. This particular responsibility means becoming a lawyer whether you like law or not, becoming a banker whether you can stomach banking or not, becoming a historian even if history makes you gag, and becoming both a researcher and a journalist, because you have to keep up with the ever-changing game board that is the globe rotating under your feet.

It means either being a wolf or a shepherd, because you cannot be a sheep after such an education. Francis is the last Pope we shall serve. We've been Good Shepherds for the innocent and helpless people of the world, but we might have been predators just as well. This is a matter of individual choice, and it bears consequences no matter what you do.

For those who have a conscience and who prefer to sleep at night and to look at themselves in mirrors without wincing, being a Good Shepherd works best. For the one in 25 among us who couldn't care less who they hurt, how much, or for what venal reasons, being a predator may be the only option, because such animals (and you know who you are) see innocence as ignorance, see weakness as opportunity, see goodness of any kind as an excuse for contempt, and purity as an excuse to despoil it.

Just be aware — there are 24 shepherds to every wolf and 390 million increasingly disgusted Americans poised to take out the entire Puerto Rican Navy.

11. Why did you include Pat Dougherty, the Managing Editor of The Anchorage Daily News, to receive a FINAL NOTICE? He's not a politician or a public employee or a banker or a judge, so it doesn't appear to make sense?

Go to The Anchorage Daily News archives and look at the first ad in the Legal Notices Section of the October 1, 2013 edition under high magnification. Write down the words that you actually see printed there and compare them to the words that **appear** to be printed on that page when you are reading this ad without the aid of a strong magnifying glass.

We believe that it will be self-explanatory, and if it isn't, we have many actual copies of all the publications of this specific Notice archived around the world for your inspection. The actual copies published as part of The Anchorage Daily News on that date show a very peculiar thing: the words that **appear to be** on the page aren't actually there. At high magnification, it becomes apparent that an entirely different and diabolical message is embedded in the page. **This is another fraudulent use of microprint to void the actual lawful notice, similar to the use of microprint on "personal" checks, replacing what appears to be merely a line for your signature with a line of**

microprint that designates your signature as an "authorizing" signature, not an *issuing* signature — which changes your presumed status from that of a beneficiary to that of an employee.

That ad and two similar prior ads were placed in the paper in behalf of the People of Alaska, as Legal Notice to the politicians, judges, bankers, corporate officers, social planners and others scheming to injure and defraud their neighbors in the upcoming game of national bankruptcy. The ad ran three times, and each time, the print staff at The Anchorage Daily News **corrupted it** in such a way that the perpetrators of all this fraud can technically claim that the clearly intended Public Notice was never delivered, and that instead, the underlying distorted and diabolical message was published instead. After all, they will argue among themselves and slap each other on the back for such cleverness — the Sheep will never catch on — and it's the ink on the page that counts, not the ink that *seems* to be on the page.

Or is it? We, the Shepherds, have something to say about that — and it is merely this: **fraud vitiates everything.** The intent to publish and the act of publishing the Notice stands as originally written and **delivered by the Post Office**.

Pat Dougherty has a commercial responsibility to provide his advertisers with good faith service, especially those who place ads in the Legal Notices section of the newspaper. By allowing distortion of the *actual* content of Legal Notices via the use of puerile optical illusions, he does great disservice to everyone involved and he assists in preserving the ongoing criminality instead of pulling an oar to straighten it out. It's true that those responsible for all this corruption and graft have lied to the members of the Fourth Estate just as they have lied to everyone else, but an editor bears responsibility for what appears — or fails to appear — in the Legal Notices.

That's why Pat Dougherty got a NOTICE of default. The Anchorage Daily News charged for a legal notice that was never actually published. This is certainly commercial default, and as he is responsible for what goes on in the press room, administrative default with respect to public obligations and functions that the newspaper holds under contract as the agency responsible for publication of Legal Notices in Alaska.

12. I am confused with all these names that are so similar meaning different things. Can you explain in a simple way?

The American Republic:

The United States of America (major) = the united States of America = uSA = 50 States joined in perpetual Union by the Articles of Confederation via the Northwest Ordinance and the Equal Footing Doctrine = organic geographically described states = living inhabitants = American Nationals = john-quincy:doe or John Quincy of the Family Doe = names of living people = heirs; beneficiaries; entitlement holders; priority creditors = private sector = Law of the Land = The Constitution for the united States of America = The United States of America in Congress Assembled = congress of the United States of America = unincorporated Trust Management Company doing business as The United States = Body Politic = senate = house of representatives = civil government = full commercial liability = sovereign nation = American Nationals = Natural and Unalienable rights = U.S. Trust = American Common Law = U.S. dollar = Public Laws = Full Enactment Clauses = State Governors; as in "Maine State Governor".

The American Democracy

The United States of America (minor) = USA = the corporate United States = the District of Columbia = Washington, D.C. = Municipal government of the District

of Columbia plus federal possessions, territories and enclaves = Seven Insular States = incorporated legal fiction entity d.b.a. the United States of America, Inc. chartered in Delaware = corporate privileges = By Laws published as "the Constitution of the United States of America" = US citizens = US Trust = "union of American states" allowed by Insular Tariff cases = US Congress operating as an oligarchy = Senate = House of Representatives = statutory (maritime) law a.k.a. "special admiralty" = Trust Management Organization doing business as "the United States of America, Inc." = jurisdiction of the high seas and navigable inland waters = operates as a commercial entity, not a Body Politic, nor a sovereign nation = Civil Rights held as privileges bestowed by or taken away by US Congress = Federal Code = limited liability = private corporation operating franchises and providing services through agencies under contract = claims to "stand for" the Republic = Public Policy = "Acts" of Congress without Enactment Clauses = public franchises organized as *foreign situs* trusts doing business under the Names of living Americans = Names using Upper and Lower case style conventions, e.g., John Quincy Adams = US Dollar = vessels in commerce = Law of the Dead – Probate Law, Administrative Law = State of state corporate municipal franchises as in "State of Ohio" = Governor of Ohio = U.S. Department of the Treasury = U.S. Department of Commerce = U.S. Department of Transportation... etc., etc., etc.

The UNITED STATES

Regional Subsidiary of the UNITED NATIONS d.b.a. UNITED STATES, INC. = 57 American "states" = French commercial corporation = secondary governmental services contractor operated by the International Monetary Fund, an agency of the United Nations, an independent international city-state located in New York State = international commercial union = Puerto Rican *Cestui Que Vie* ESTATE trusts operated as franchises of the UNITED STATES, INC. under the NAMES of living Americans = "JOHN QUINCY ADAMS" = international law = Law of the Sea = Admiralty = US CITIZENS = US TRUST = CONSTITUTION OF THE UNITED STATES = US DOLLAR = US DISTRICT COURT = UNITED STATES SENATE = PRESIDENT OBAMA = UNITED STATES HOUSE OF REPRESENTATIVES = UNITED STATES CONGRESS = ACTS OF CONGRESS = STATE OF OHIO = GOVERNOR OF OHIO = US TREASURY DEPARTMENT = INTERNAL REVENUE SERVICE... etc, etc., etc.

Whenever you see names in all small letters or when you see entities physically described, you are talking about the **Republic** and the real world of living people and private property and valid contracts. All **real assets** of the nation are held in perpetual trust by the **Global Estate Trust**. The trials and tribulations of individual Trust Management Organizations are never supposed to affect any asset held in trust. Thus, the name **"nelly-jo: blanchard"** is the name of a living female. So is "Nelly-Jo **of the family** Blanchard" a valid way to designate a living female. A US dollar is a known weight of silver refined to a stated quality. The Georgia State has known geographical borders. But, **Nelly Jo Blanchard** is a *foreign situs trust* created and owned under conditions of deceit and non-disclosure by agencies of the State of Georgia, a *franchise* of the United States of America, Inc., which is owned and operated as a business by the Federal Reserve, Inc. which are incorporated in turn under the auspices of the United States of America (**minor**). In the same way, **NELLY JO BLANCHARD** is a foreign (Puerto Rican) ESTATE Trust — a Roman Inferior Trust — created, owned, and operated under conditions of non-disclosure and deceit by the International

Monetary Fund (IMF) which is an agency of the UNITED NATIONS, INC., operating under the auspices of the United Nations, an independent, international **city-state**.

When you see names styled in Upper and Lower Case, you are talking about incorporated entities known as *"legal fiction entities"* spawned by the United States of America (**minor**) or one of its corporate municipal franchises, such as the State of Alaska, which exist only on paper, are subject to their charter, and enjoy certain immoral advantages in commerce. **Nelly Jo Blanchard** is the Name of a *foreign situs* **trust** created by agents of the United States of America, Inc., to function as a *"commercial vessel"* and to act as a surety for their own corporate debts — without the knowledge or consent of the similarly named living American. **"Nelly Jo Blanchard"** is a *foreign situs* trust claimed and owned as chattel by the Federal Reserve Banks doing business as the United States of America, Inc. **These entities are in fact abusing the legal conventions which apply to naming corporate entities and making a *de facto* false claim by using a small "t" in describing themselves as "the United States of America" and doing so by claiming to represent BOTH the 50 states and the 7 insular states. This adds to the confusion as to who is who and what is what.**

When you see NAMES styled in all UPPER CASE letters, you are talking about *additional incorporated entities* spawned by the UNITED STATES, a regional subsidiary of the UNITED NATIONS, chartered in Puerto Rico, operated as franchises, agencies and subsidiaries, functioning as secondary creditors in commerce and commercial vessels owned and operated by the International Monetary Fund. **"NELLY JO BLANCHARD"** is a Roman Inferior Trust (also known as a Cestui Que Vie Trust) operated out of Puerto Rico by the IMF doing business as the UNITED STATES, INC. and all under the auspices of the UNITED NATIONS, INC. which is in turn organized under the authority of the United Nations acting as a separate independent and international **city-state**.

The next stage of this endless fraud is now beginning, with conversion of the IMF owned and operated ESTATE trusts into transmitting utilities owned and operated by a new UN subsidiary calling itself the FEDERAL RESERVE. This entity is creating yet another bunch of legal fiction entities under names styled in this form: "JOHN Q. PUBLIC" and all named after living Americans.

This entire con game is based on non-disclosure and semantic deceits and is a form of sophisticated identity theft carried out via abuse of the rights of usufruct exercised by Trust Management Organizations acting in Breach of Trust — **all done by organizations which owe to the victims absolute fiduciary accountability.**

13. Do you mean that when I get a tax notice from the IRS addressed to my NAME, it isn't actually addressed to me?

Precisely. It is addressed to a Puerto Rican ESTATE Trust and you are presumed to be a federal official — specifically, a federal contracting officer known as a "Withholding Agent" working for the government of the United States of America (minor) who is responsible for administering this ESTATE as a civil executor. Every time you sign a 1040 or a 1065 or other federal tax document, claiming to be a Withholding Agent, *you obligate yourself* to act as a "US citizen" subject to every jot of Federal Code, including the 120,000-plus pages of gobbledygook known as the Internal Revenue Code, plus whatever whims the US Congress may have next week. Withholding Agents are responsible for collecting and withholding taxes on *revenues imported* to Puerto Rico.

The perpetrators tax you for the privilege of *donating your money* to a Puerto Rican ESTATE Trust operated under your name by the IMF — which you do every time you *deposit money* in an account belonging to YOUR NAME IN CAPITAL LETTERS thereby "voluntarily" converting your own *private property* into corporate income and also *accrue the import tax* due for importing revenue to a Puerto Rican Trust.

They operate a monopoly on legal tender such that you have no valid means to pay a debt, then prevent you from *discharging* any debt — **which is the only remedy they provided to justify their monopoly on legal tender** — and then they tax you for the *privilege* of donating the I.O.U.'s they foisted off on you in the first place to a Puerto Rican ESTATE trust operated in your name.

Next, if you let them get away with it, the new FEDERAL RESERVE will subtly change the NAME on "your" ESTATE account, changing it to this form: JOHN Q. PUBLIC, which is a transmitting utility — yet another legal fiction entity created out of thin-air and operated under a "similar name" — and they will happily make false claims of debt and ownership against this entity, too.

All the gold that the United States of America, Inc., stole from your grandparents in the 1930's will now be used to issue a "new currency" backed with gold and silver — gold and silver they seized under force of arms from your families to begin with, and never paid back — **and the new "US Treasury Notes", like the "Federal Reserve Notes" will still be mere I.O.U.'s that further indebt you every time you use them to "pay" a debt.**

14. So What is the bottom line of all this?

There is either a contract between the governmental service providers, or there is no contract for services in play. If there is a contract, they have to abide by it. If there isn't a contract, nobody is obligated to pay the providers for any services provided, and in this case, those providing the services additionally become recognizable as foreigners without any cause to be on American soil, therefore subject to deportation and confiscation of their assets.

The only valid contract ever established between the American states and the **Global Estate Trust**, is the Original Equity Contract known as The Constitution for the united States of America. The purported changes made in 1871 and the "new" Constitution published at that time pertained only to the United States of America (minor) and was never fully disclosed and never properly ratified as anything wider ranging, with the result that all the changes made in 1913 and 1933 were never fully disclosed and never ratified by the states, either.

The documents known as "the Constitution of the United States of America" published in 1871 and the more recent "Constitution of the United States" have no meaning outside the narrow confines of the United States of America (minor) and the incorporated entities that created these documents. They hold no water in international commerce. They have no valid basis as international treaties between the United States of America (minor) and The United States of America (major).

The only contract binding the American states to the Global Estate Trust remains as the over-200-year-old Constitution for the united States of America, and that is the contract that must be performed upon, if any contract exists at all.

It is "one way or the other" from an international treaty and commercial contract standpoint — either there is a contract that must be honored, or there is no contract and these freebooters need to be removed from American shores and their false claims need to be repudiated. **This is precisely the viewpoint that the Pope is obligated to take as the Trustee responsible for the administration of the Global Estate Trust as a whole, and it is the stand he has taken.**

In enforcing the original equity contract, the Pope can call upon all the other members of the **Global Estate Trust** — over 200 countries — and he will have many willing supporters if he is forced to take action against the present leadership of the United States of America (minor) d.b.a. PRESIDENT BARACK H. OBAMA and the US CONGRESS.

Both Russia and China have already pledged their support to impose economic and military sanctions if the criminal banking cartels presently operating the American government don't back down and restore the commodity-based monetary system; agree to implement Basel III banking protocols; stop rigging the commodity markets; and take other steps to ensure global security and prosperity.

It is in the best interests of everyone on earth outside a very narrow group of politicians, bankers, lawyers, military officers, and corrupt churchmen, to bring the present criminality to a halt, so therefore, one way or another, it will be done.

The Pope has no choice, and neither do you.

The bottom line can be summed up in one question to be answered — is there a contract or not? If so, that contract must be honored. If not, the employees of the United States of America (minor) and the United Nations are out of a job and those who knowingly promoted the fraud are to be prosecuted as criminals and deported.

15. What is the status of an American facing the present court system?

There are only two possibilities currently being entertained by American Bar Association members, as a consequence of the shakedown put in place by the Roosevelt Administration eighty years ago, following the *Erie Railroad v. Thompkins* case: they are either (1) addressing an in-house administrative corporate tribunal to provide information or make a claim against the United States of America (minor) or one of its municipal franchises or agencies per the Administrative Procedures Act, or they are (2) facing a foreign maritime court and acting under a burden of undisclosed false presumption — except in the very few cases where an actual maritime issue and contract exists.

These are the only possibilities and the members of the American Bar Association fight hard to ignore or weasel out of ever admitting that they are functioning in either capacity.

There is no such thing under the current system as a State Statute. There isn't a single valid Enactment Clause anywhere to be seen in the volumes of "statute" published by the "State of Alaska", nor is there any power of enactment within the Administrative Code of the STATE OF ALASKA.

Anyone properly trained in the practice of law has only to glance at these documents to know they are private in-house publications. Unfortunately, two generations of American lawyers have been purposefully left in ignorance as pernicious as that inflicted on the general populace.

This ignorance better serves the purposes of the "Court Administrators" who are employees by the same banks that have perpetuated the gross fraud and criminality engulfing the monetary system, the banking system, the political system, and the government both federal and state.

The perpetrators have gone so far as to openly and publically declare in the Foreign Sovereign Immunity Act and the International Organizations Immunity Act that all state offices have been relinquished to the UN and all state law has been released to international venues, so even by their own admission, there is no opportunity to question these facts. It is all public record.

All the administrative "law" practiced by the courts in America is Roman Civil Law created under the auspices of the Roman Curia and transplanted as the law form chosen by the international bankruptcy trustees to administer the bankruptcy of the United States of America, Inc.

All the maritime law practiced by the STATE OF ALASKA courts is "Special Admiralty"— a gobbledygook created and adopted to allow perverse presumptions of maritime association and contract in civil cases involving *foreign situs* trusts created by the United States of America (minor) that are merely **presumed to be** sureties for the debts of the bankrupt Trust Management Organization d.b.a. United States of America, Inc. — and all washed down with ample and outrageous probate fraud.

According to the perpetrators, the "vessel" they created, a *foreign situs* trust belonging to the State of Alaska franchise of the bankrupt United States of America, Inc., went missing years ago. John Quincy Adams hasn't been heard from, or so they claim, so he has been presumed dead and his estate has been rolled over into a Puerto Rican ESTATE trust operating under the name JOHN QUINCY ADAMS.

This is venal probate fraud of the worst sort, carried out systematically against an unsuspecting and peaceful populace of civilian inhabitants of the land, people who are owed the full protection of their International Trustees; the Pope and HRM Elizabeth II; and the good faith and service of their **employees** under commercial contract to provide governmental services.

All the admiralty law practiced by the US DISTRICT COURT is international Law Merchant falsely transplanted without contract or consent, usurped upon the land and used against the unwitting American people with devastating effect upon them and their fraudulently constructed ESTATES in flagrant violation of the Treaties of Westminster.

There are at present **no** formal courts in America serving **living** Americans at all. The only way a living American can appear is via Special Appearance — a status akin to a ghost who may be heard and seen, but without standing.

To address any court in America with standing, a living American has two choices: (1) to reclaim controlling interest in their ESTATE according to the ancient laws governing Roman Inferior Trusts —which throws a mighty monkey wrench into a "court system" that is not designed to deal with civil American executors, or (2) to create an American *inter vivos* trust operating under a separate legal name which is competent to address commercial issues in an international public venue.

Living Americans are owed the American Common Law, and as we've already seen, the American Bar Association has acted under a fraudulent administrative order to **only** operate in administrative and maritime (international) venues, since 1938.

Without overturning this administrative protocol, the courts CANNOT function lawfully in the vast majority of cases, so they do not function lawfully. They function as described herein, as criminal ventures, rigged gambling syndicates, operating for-profit prisons that are "guaranteed full occupancy by contract", etc.

16. If the federal government is a private, for-profit Trust Management Organization, providing governmental services as a corporation with a lot of "STATE" franchises, like Burger King, International — what does that mean for the "STATE" legislatures?

It means that they are committing major league constructive fraud. They have no "legislative power" outside of the private affairs of their own deceptively named corporation, no valid claim to the American national trust assets, no valid claim upon the American states, no controlling interest in the states, and certainly no controlling interest in the private assets of the American people.

They cannot even claim to represent anyone but the small percentage of those who bother to vote, AND, who voted for them, individually — a matter which cannot be proven with a secret ballot. **All these people claiming to "represent" others, can't prove that they represent anybody at all.** At best, they can round up a group of family and friends who will swear that they voted for them in the most recent election.

Grandma Grace and Uncle Henry notwithstanding, with less than 30% of the populace voting, there is no way for the most popular politicians in Juneau, or Washington, DC, to claim that they represent a majority controlling interest of any kind.

As a practical matter, every member of the current "US CONGRESS" and every member of the STATE OF _____ LEGISLATURE is operating as an *international criminal* engaged in fraud and identity theft and they are impersonating American officials — whether they know it or not.

The Alaska State operates under the Alaska Statehood Compact.

It is **foreign** with respect to the State of Alaska and also **foreign** with respect to the STATE OF ALASKA. Those who are operating these private, for-profit corporations in violation of their corporate charters and in violation of the public trust, have cause to know that they are NOT the government of the Alaska State, and that they do NOT have any controlling interest in the assets of Alaska State.

Note: it is the "Alaska State Capitol Building" — not the "State of Alaska Capitol Building". These interlopers are occupying public buildings and impersonating public officials like a flock of starlings stealing the nests of better birds, and the fact that most of them — like most of their constituents — are totally ignorant of this fact, does not alter the situation at all.

17. What can be done to correct this situation?

As a first step... American Nationals can operate their own courts. They are not obligated to depend upon BAR accredited attorneys for anything, and would do well not to hire them except under very narrowly defined "limited" Power of Attorney to act as agents, not representatives.

The original equity contract includes the creation of a Grand Jury system which is meant to operate as a Fourth Branch of government, serving to present charges against those guilty of crimes and misdemeanors against the living inhabitants of the 50 states.

Qualified Grand Jurors volunteer to serve as part of a statewide or county jury pool and may investigate any allegation of criminal or civil wrong-doing which comes to their attention. Following due process, they are enabled to present either indictments (against US citizens) or present charges (against American Nationals).

Trial juries may be convened by any elected county sheriff or by a U.S. marshal (note the small "m") or elected county judge — who does not have to be a member of the Bar Association. The U.S. marshals are under contract to protect the U.S. Mail and are the only "federal" law enforcement officers commissioned to act as constitutional officers. They have free egress on the land of the 50 states United when engaged in the performance of their duties. All other similarly named offices operated as "US Marshals" or "US MARSHALS" are private and non-constitutional agency positions that enjoy no special status or granted access on the land of the 50 states United, similar to NSA, BATF, IRS, FBI, and DEA officers. In a few remaining locations, notably in Alaska, there are as yet no fully functioning counties and the U.S. marshals, Provost marshals, civil postmasters, and notary publics serve as the constitutional officers.

All US Marshals and US MARSHALS can be "invoked" to occupy the constitutional office of U.S. marshal by explicitly addressing them in this capacity and requesting them to function in that office. A similar situation exists when requesting service from a notary public, postmaster, or provost marshal. The same individual can be called upon to function in both public and private offices, and are required to do so, though they are seldom fully advised or trained in their responsibilities as constitutional officers.

American Nationals can also demand that all persons elected to public office fill those offices immediately, under oath, in **unincorporated** capacity, and function in that capacity **exclusively** for the duration of their term in office. This requires them to accept full commercial liability for their actions and to function with full fiduciary obligation to the people of the state. They can then no longer play the game of "Which hat am I wearing now?" and function in conflict of interest, plundering the assets of the organic state and the living people for private banking and other corporate interests while claiming to "represent" those same people and states.

Americans can also operate their unincorporated state legislatures to enforce and update the actual Constitution for the united States of America, by a process of ratified amendment undertaken by properly informed and seated **unincorporated** state legislatures, and a national referendum of the **unincorporated** Body Politic composed of living people — bearing in mind that **this document has not been altered since December of 1865** — or we can negotiate a totally new contract with the **Global Estate Trust**, but given the present state of general ignorance, that would hardly be advisaable to do.

Those who are nominally occupying public office need to act with propriety for now and limit their actions to those appropriate for **employees** of the Alaska State and the Alaskan People. Those who are members of the Alaska Bar Association need to demand immediate, drastic, and unequivocal administrative change — or tear up their BAR Cards and start their own club operating real American Courts under real American Common Law.

18. This whole situation makes me feel terrified and out of control. Why are you so cool and calm?

The Pope is determined to do the right thing and he is doing it, despite wild accusations, despite false claims, despite a very vile propaganda campaign launched against him personally and against the Roman Catholic Church by globalist bank operatives. With more than a billion members worldwide, the Church is one of the largest Body Politics on earth and its membership cuts across all racial and national boundaries. There are also more than two billion people with a direct interest in correcting this situation, including the entire combined populations of North and South America, Canada, Australia, Japan, and most of Europe. Americans are not in this stew pot alone. What happens to us, happens to everyone else caught in the same system. This includes the perpetrators and their home bases — globally. The reckoning is coming too fast for them to move their operations far enough. The globe has become too small.

Under international law, however, Americans are unique in that the entire civil government is vested in each and every living man and woman born on American soil. Americans, quite literally, are sovereigns on the land. The lowliest file clerk in America has more **civil** authority than the entire federal government, so there is no lack of civil government in America, and never has been.

Any claim that the civil government has not operated since 1865, due to the fact that a properly seated and functioning congress has not acted since then, is immediately rendered null and void by the simple fact that sovereigns upon the land are **not obligated** to convene a congress or any other legislative body. We can do what we like, but we must now recognize that our failure to operate our civil government has created a vacuum of power that unscrupulous men have taken advantage of. Our counties, the basic building blocks of the American civil government, must be rebuilt and redirected to function properly at a grassroots level. Usurpation onto the land by "boroughs" and "municipalities" existing under "federal" charters — that is, under the auspices of the United States of America (minor) or the United Nations City State — which are **foreign nations creating unauthorized settlements on our land** — must be stopped, and the existing charters of municipalities like DETROIT must be voided as criminal personage carried out by foreign powers against the state of Michigan and its people.

Some individual states have given these freebooters asylum, including the states of Virginia, Maryland, Delaware, and New York. By so doing, they have allowed *foreign nations* to take root and operate on our shores, to the detriment of all Americans. The states of Delaware, Maryland, and Missouri have all knowingly allowed the proliferation of *foreign corporations* using names overtly designed to mimmick and be confused with The United States of America (major), other states, federal and state agencies, and a plethora of other entities. In so doing, they have helped promote and promulgate this entire fraud scheme. Their state legislatures are culpable and answerable to the other states with which they are joined in perpetual union.

Americans are blessed in that they have been taught the Great Laws of the Bible. They know the essence of justice, so they are competent to self-govern. **The premise of American Common Law is simple enough for a child to understand — do no harm** — and if and when you do, make amends. American Common Law is simple in this respect: if there's no victim; there is no crime.

All American Nationals when improperly addressed by one of these foreign admiralty courts should ask five questions:

1. Where is the alleged **maritime** contract? These courts have no jurisdiction more than a mile inland.

2. Who or what is being addressed as the DEFENDANT? (Is this a trust? It can't be a living man since the name is in all capital of the dead).

3. Is this court a constitutional entity? (If so, is it an Article 3 or Article 5 court? Since it has to be one of the two. Most "JUDGES" will vacate at this point).

4. Where is the Injured Party, named as PLAINTIFF? (It's not a living man or woman, so what is it? Who owns it? Who is responsible for it?)

5. What jurisdiction or authority does this court or its officers have to address fraudulent claims to my attention? (If the documents were mailed, they committed mail fraud. If they were hand delivered, they trespassed on private property).

The 80 million or more regulations, statutes and codes that the incorporated Trust Management Organizations have created for themselves, their employees, and their "citizens", do not apply to Americans. So under what authority do these Cretins continue to assert, that they do?

As for the claim that Americans fall under the "exclusive legislative" control of the United States of America (minor) via its establishment of "state" franchises, all the claim accomplished was attempted identity theft. The same for any claim made by the United Nations. All claims of "war powers" and "national emergency" apply only to the corporate United States and no such powers and emergencies have existed within or by The United States of America.

The bankers beneath this criminality can, potentially, cause destruction and havoc, but in the end they will lose, along with everyone else, if they do, and they have more to lose. Even the arms dealers and Mafiosi and drug lords can ill-afford to lose their American Hemisphere estate and American investments and American bases of operation. The bad guys can only shoot themselves in the foot.

They will either allow an orderly return to American self-government under American law and a real dollar, or they can find a nice new home some non-aligned nation. Their flight to "UN protection" will not ultimately help them. That has already been decided by the Pope and Global Estate Trustees.

As for any claims of a military coup and defining the presence of the US Army on American soil, as a "foreign occupation" by the United States of America (minor), such claims do not stand up in the international community. **First**, then-President Andrew Jackson made three public declarations officially ending the Civil War. **Second**, even if it is under the direction of the President of the United States when it comes to defending The United States of America, the US Army is paid for its services under contract. Any action undertaken by the US Army against American Nationals on the land of the 50 states United, would be a blatant commercial crime, and the United Nations could ill afford a reputation for allowing that.

Finally, the Pope's recent admonishment of the Italian Mafiosi, is not devoid of meaning for them, and the messages going out worldwide to the administrators of the Crown Temple, have similar meaning for its recipients.

This is why we are cool and calm — as stated in the FINAL NOTICE, all these issues, claims, and considerations have been deliberated upon and decided, at the highest levels of international governance.

19. All these "legislatures" and public officials have been using public resources, buildings and everything else

to benefit their own private for-profit corporations, for DECADES. They've sold off billions of dollars worth of Alaska's oil for pennies on the dollar to their cronies in the oil companies, siphoned off billions into slush funds not accounted for, by impersonating American public officials and asserting a controlling interest in the assets of the organic states . . . that's what you're telling me?

Yes. In 1946 the "federal government" — a private, for profit, mostly foreign-owned corporation under contract to provide governmental services — adopted a crooked bookkeeping system and the "US CONGRESS" declared it legal for the government, although illegal for everyone else.

They borrowed the "double entry bookkeeping system" from Fast Eddie O'Hara, who was Al Capone's bookkeeper. The IRS learned it from Eddie when they prosecuted Capone back in the 1920's. Getting rid of this system has been the principle driving force behind all the Basel I, II, and III banking reforms.

The essence of the crooked government accounting is in keeping two sets of books, use of undisclosed "off book" escrow accounts, undeclared income accounts, and "future time encumbrances". They have also failed to transparently report their "public investments" to the public.

To use an example from Alaska — the STATE OF ALASKA splits its income streams into "budgeted" and "non-budgeted" income. The GOVERNOR decides how much he wants to give out as a budget and the LEGISLATURE argues over this little bone and keeps the crowds entertained for the rest of the session. **This sideshow keeps attention focused only on the budgeted amount.** Meanwhile, the far greater share of the income and investment is being "passed through" to investment accounts and escrow accounts and subsidiary accounts belonging to technically separate agencies.

Once a year the STATE OF ALASKA produces a financial report called the COMPREHENSIVE ANNUAL FINANCIAL REPORT — the CAFR. This is far from a true "comprehensive" financial report, in that it passes off responsibility for including the detailed data from all the ANNUAL FINANCIAL REPORTS of entities like the ALASKA MENTAL HEALTH TRUST and the ALASKA HOUSING FINANCE CORPORATION and the UNIVERSITY OF ALASKA and so on, but it does reveal some very startling things and it provides the basis to dig out the truth about STATE OF ALASKA finances.

The last time this sort of analysis was done was in the 1990's and it was only a "big strokes" research project. It did not get down to the fine detail level, nor did it exhaustively investigate myriad subsidiary ANNUAL FINANCIAL REPORTS, only the three largest ones at that time. The STATE OF ALASKA had over $3 trillion dollars in unreported "non-budgeted" income, interest, investments from prior years, other investment income, program fees, and monetized assets standing on the books. Only the COMMISSIONER OF REVENUE, LINDSEY GOLDBERG, THE GOVERNOR'S OFFICE, and senior bureaucrats at LEGISLATIVE BUDGET AND AUDIT would have an accurate guess how much it has ratted away now.

This is typical of the way these corporations work. They keep people distracted by focusing public attention on the pennies in one pocket while they are stealing the gold bars from the other pocket.

As an example of the corporate conflict of interest — the leadership of the "STATE OF ALASKA LEGISLATURE" and various other corporate players have been happily colluding to squeeze-play the Alaskan people out of the benefit of their natural gas resources. The STATE OF ALASKA has long owned via investment a very large interest in ENSTAR NATURAL GAS and has a vested interest in maintaining ENSTAR's monopoly as the only viable gas supply utility in Alaska. So, as a self-interested private corporation, the STATE OF ALASKA is determined to keep the price of natural gas and propane in Alaska unnaturally high, to help maintain ENSTAR'S monopoly on in-state gas energy supplies, and to prevent any large scale development of Alaska's gas resources that would encourage competition for ENSTAR. It also has a vested self-interest in wrangling pipeline construction contracts for ENSTAR.

This is an especially choice investment for the STATE OF ALASKA because public utilities are regulated and thereby **guaranteed** a 12% above cost profit, no matter what the costs of a project may be. All the cost in such a venture gets passed on to the consumers, and the perpetrators get a 12% profit **no matter what**.

The STATE OF ALASKA corporate leadership is willing to consider a wildly expensive small or medium diameter gas pipeline that guarantees extremely high consumer gas prices in Alaska for decades to come — because that option (1) guarantees ENSTAR's monopoly for decades to come, (2) guarantees top prices for propane delivered in-state for decades to come, and (3) guarantees a 12% **above cost** profit for ENSTAR — and the STATE OF ALASKA **no matter what the costs of construction are** — for every mile of pipe the company lays.

This situation neatly demonstrates the conflict of interest which exists all across the board when private for-profit corporations are allowed to assume a controlling interest in public assets. They have a built-in and constant temptation to operate in favor of their own bottom line at the expense of the organic states and the people they are obligated by fiduciary trust to serve.

This gas development plan to construct a small or medium diameter gas pipeline is perfectly desirable from the standpoint of the STATE OF ALASKA'S bottom line, but it betrays and victimizes the actual beneficiaries of the Alaska Trust, the ones who should be benefited first and most of all by Alaska's resources.

This calculated breach of public trust for private profit is on top of the theft of identity and credit that has already been described, and it goes on in every STATE franchise, not just the STATE OF ALASKA.

The take home message to members of the STATE OF ALASKA LEGISLATURE is that the organization is already in gross violation of its charter, in violation of the public trust, acting in breach of trust, engaging in felony fraud, acting with gross fiduciary malfeasance, and cannot make up for the past. Billions upon billions of dollars have been stolen and wasted, misdirected, poorly invested for petty, selfish reasons, and siphoned off by the STATE OF ALASKA.

A new dialogue must begin, and in the meantime, those occupying corporate offices need to be very mindful of the limitations, temptations, and actual nature of their elected office within a private corporation under contract to provide stipulated governmental services. They must also be aware that they have no valid controlling interest in the assets of the Alaska State and that they have failed to perform according to the Alaska Statehood Compact, which potentially voids all contracts for all services and all contracts which the STATE OF ALASKA has or has entered into since 1959.

As an example of the same phenomenon at the national level, the "US Congress" recently passed the Dodd-Frank Act, gratuitously granting itself the right to confiscate money deposited in bank accounts properly belonging to American Nationals. Unknown to those Americans, the banks have secretively practiced unlawful conversion against them and what they think of as their bank accounts have all been established instead in the name of Puerto Rican Estate Trusts that are under the control of the corporate United States. Poor old john-quincy:adams has been "donating" all his credit accruals in the form of his checking

117

and savings and demand deposits and mortgage escrow holdings and everything else to benefit John Quincy Adams, and that long-lost beneficiary's Estate has been rolled over into an ESTATE trust doing business under "his" NAME — JOHN QUINCY ADAMS, which actually owns and controls all the bank accounts.

Don't worry if you get dizzy trying to follow all the semantic deceit. It's all fraud, top to bottom and front to back, null and void, unlawful, illegal, and criminal without excuse. The point is that Senators Dodd and Frank thought it was perfectly all right to bilk the American people out of their life savings and retirement accounts — and they did this while overtly claiming to "represent" the victims and their estates.

The men and women sitting as officers of both the United States of America, Inc. and the UNITED STATES, INC. feel secure committing these and other heinous commercial crimes against Americans, because technically, they are not Americans anymore. Once they took their oath of office, they came under the protection of the corporate United States and the United Nations and they claim "immunity" for all their acts.

Unfortunately for them, fraud is a crime on an international basis, and any incorporated entity, whether it purports itself to be a nation, a state, or the local D.Q. franchise, is subject to dissolution for violation of its charter and for actions identifying it as a criminal syndicate. The officers of a criminal syndicate are readily exposed without the benefit of any corporate veil or diplomatic immunity.

20. You have put your own private assets at risk to pursue justice and correction of all these circumstances. You stated in the FINAL NOTICE that THE SUPERIOR COURT FOR THE STATE OF ALASKA owes you "reparations" and damages in the amount of $1,600,000.00 and that the STATE OF ALASKA stands subject to dissolution as a result. How is all this possible? Wasn't the

<u>property foreclosed for not paying a commercial mortgage?</u>

Fraud vitiates everything and it makes no difference who the fraudsters are, or, in this case, who they pretend to be. No "courts" in America have valid jurisdiction over us or our private property, including the **private** trusts recorded as the actual owners of the property in question.

The reparations result from damage done to us and our estate by the corporate United States and its franchises operated as "States" and the damage claim further results from the STATE OF ALASKA's failure to monitor and control the operations of THE SUPERIOR DISTRICT COURT FOR THE STATE OF ALASKA.

Technically, under the Law of the Sea, we could claim 800 times the loss as damages, but that represents precisely the kind of cut-throat and unreasonable piracy we seek to end. The actual material damage to our joint estate trust is currently and fairly estimated at $1,600,000.00 USD and that reasonable and limited amount is what we have claimed.

THE SUPERIOR COURT FOR THE STATE OF ALASKA is a private, for-profit, non-governmental entity operated by the ALASKA COURT SYSTEM, INC. which is operated by the FEDERAL RESERVE. As described earlier, the CLERK set up a docket number and penal bonds and "deposited" the case as a security in the DALLAS FEDERAL RESERVE BANK. JUDGE PAUL OLSON received the converted security making the COURT the creditor and ruled in favor of — guess who? The COURT and the COURT's employer, the FEDERAL RESERVE. This is gross conflict of interest, unlawful conversion, insider trading, etc. — but it is also fraud in name and deed.

Just as the corporate United States claims to stand for **The** United States of America, THE SUPERIOR DISTRICT COURT FOR THE STATE OF ALASKA is deceptively named to imply that it operates under the auspices of the STATE OF ALASKA. It does not, and the ATTORNEY GENERAL for the STATE OF ALASKA will very quickly confirm this. THE SUPERIOR DISTRICT COURT **FOR** THE STATE OF ALASKA is a private for-profit debt collection agency and the only thing the "for" in its name implies is that Alaska is its geographically defined place of operations.

The STATE OF ALASKA's failure is that it has not honored its obligation to protect the assets of the national and state trusts. As a franchise of the UNITED STATES, INC. which inherited the trust obligations along with the juicy service contracts that it has administered throughout the bankruptcy reorganization of the United States of America, Inc., the STATE OF ALASKA was a successor trustee.

The STATE OF ALASKA = bankruptcy trustee of the "State of Alaska" = trustee of the Alaska State, and as any mathematician knows, equivalencies work both ways. Although the so-called "national bankruptcy" of the old Trust Management Organization has been settled as of July 1, 2013, it was still ongoing at the time the demonstration cases were prosecuted, and no matter how the ATTORNEY GENERAL tries to side-step the issue, both the redeemed ESTATE trusts and the actual title holder, an American express *inter vivos* trust, were and are owed his protection.

Our rights and private property assets are all part of the national trust and like assets held in any trust, these assets are inviolate, **not subject to** claims that result from any bankruptcy of trustees — and this is true now as it was in 1933 and in 1863 and from the moment the individual organic states proclaimed their geographic boundaries as independent nation-states.

Seeking to convert our private property assets into foreign corporate assets by a process of contractual entrapment, semantic deceit, and non-disclosure is fraud, as is the hypothecation of corporate debt against our private property assets under similar conditions of deceit and non-disclosure, as is creation of property titles under color of law, as is sale of property and transfer of property titles without full disclosure, as is the use of off-book demand accounts in the administration of mortgage agreements, as is usury, as is the use of unilateral contracts, as is the use of I.O.U's as legal tender.

The STATE OF ALASKA, INC. as the local franchise of the UNITED STATES, INC. is responsible for safe-guarding our rights and those include our private property rights which have been grossly, knowingly, and self-interestedly violated by THE SUPERIOR DISTRICT COURT FOR THE STATE OF ALASKA, INC. which has acted without jurisdiction and without a valid controlling interest against declared non-combatant civilian beneficiaries and **Third Parties** to this entire circumstance.

The properties in question were **recorded** more than ten years ago with the Recorder's Office in the name of **a** single private internationally held *inter vivos* trust d.b.a. "Anna M. Riezinger-von Reitz and James C. Belcher" which was properly established in original jurisdiction many years ago to act as a viable American commercial vessel in international commercial venues. Acting under duress and to clear the titles, we additionally and momentarily donned the "Federal Contracting Officer" hat that is ours as remedy for the first round of fraud and predation unleashed by FDR and in that capacity released all "federal" liens held against the properties. By Public Policy of the United States of America, Inc. and by the Uniform Commercial Code that binds the UNITED STATES and its STATE OF ALASKA franchise, all mortgages financed by any bank operated under the auspices of any "federal" or "state" corporation providing services to us, are subject to discharge favoring the beneficiaries of the ESTATES. Those documents are also on file with the Alaska Recorder's Office.

When we presented THE SUPERIOR DISTRICT COURT FOR THE STATE OF ALASKA with copies of the Birth

Certificates of the Puerto Rican ESTATE trusts doing business as "ANNA MARIA RIEZINGER" and "JAMES CLINTON BELCHER" and presented ourselves as the living beneficiaries of these trusts, which are Cestui Que Vie Trusts, two things should have happened. First, the COURT should have inquired as to our identity in behalf of the bankruptcy trustee and required that we produce competent witnesses and supporting documentation –which in this case we provided in the form of an Ecclesiastical Deed Poll and affidavit entitled "Statement of Identity" autographed by living witnesses. Second, the COURT should have recognized that we are the lawful beneficiaries and equitable title holders of the NAMED trusts asserting a controlling interest in their assets, and the COURT should have relinquished its merely assumed position as creditor and arbiter.

When the true beneficiary of a *Cestui Que Vie* Trust appears in COURT — if it is a real "court" of any kind — it **must** collapse the trust in favor of the equitable title holder. Must. No questions asked. **THE SUPERIOR DISTRICT COURT FOR THE STATE OF ALASKA failed to do this and it violated international law in the process.**

It also revealed its nature as nothing but a glorified debt collection agency operating under conditions of open fraud and collecting moreover from innocent Third Parties under conditions of armed extortion.

The COURT's Officer, the prosecuting attorney, Michelle Boutin, hired the ALASKA STATE TROOPERS to act as mercenaries and enter our posted private property under armed force and threaten to evict us from our home and thereby extorted more than $100,000.00 from our private estate trust.

There is no practical difference between what the COURT did in our demonstration case and Don Guido demanding protection money. It's the same exact racket being carried out under the noses of the ALASKA TROOPERS who were even co-opted into providing enforcement for this, and the FBI which was notified and informed, and the U.S. marshals, who are under contract with the Universal Postal Union to protect us and prevent the mail fraud that was used to promote the COURT's actions, and the STATE OF ALASKA, the local franchise of the UNITED STATES, INC. which should have been busily protecting our interests as the known Primary Creditors of the United States of America, Inc.

We couldn't possibly owe the Federal Reserve more than the Federal Reserve already owed us, and the STATE OF ALASKA knew that, claimed to be our local representative in the US BANKRUPTCY proceedings — yet stood by, allowed this, and did nothing.

In a very real sense, we had already paid our protection money — to the STATE OF ALASKA and the STATE OF ALASKA failed to perform, which resulted in this egregious harm to us and our real property assets. Instead of honoring its contract, the STATE OF ALASKA (an IMF franchise) colluded with the ALASKA COURT SYSTEM (a FEDERAL RESERVE franchise) to attack and bilk innocent civilian Third Parties.

To recap: Our individual estates were claimed by the United States of America, Inc. under conditions of fraud and non-disclosure and via a process of identity theft and semantic deceit, were entered as sureties in their corporate bankruptcy proceedings. Our estates were then rolled into a Puerto Rican ESTATE trust operated under our NAMES by the US Bankruptcy Trustee, the Secretary of the Treasury of Puerto Rico. When we presented Special Appearance and redeemed the Birth Certificates issued to these ESTATES as Third Parties and produced proof that we are the living beneficiaries of these ESTATE trusts, the COURT employed by the FEDERAL RESERVE (we are their priority creditors) should have recognized our controlling interest immediately and should have discharged all debts accrued in the interim by those claiming to represent us.

The entire claim of the FEDERAL RESERVE operating THE SUPERIOR DISTRICT COURT FOR THE STATE OF ALASKA against our trust property is, as you can see from all the foregoing, based on a series of false claims and semantic deceits. After more than a hundred years of fraud and false claims and layers of semantic deceits, it is virtually impossible to determine who actually holds title to anything in America without recourse to the Law Merchant (modern day Uniform Commercial Code) and Law of Adverse Possession.

In the international jurisdiction that all these incorporated entities operate in, possession is nine-tenths of the law, and via our private internationally held *inter vivos* trust doing business as "Anna M. Riezinger-von Reitz and James C. Belcher" — a separate unified legally named and copyrighted entity operated in original jurisdiction — my husband and I have been in open, notorious, and unopposed possession of the property described as Lots 11 and 12, Block 2, Birch Park Subdivision in Big Lake, Alaska, for more than ten (10) years, and have undertaken all the improvements thereon without exception. By adverse possession in international admiralty and also according to "statute" adopted by the corporations responsible for attacking us and published as their "law" — the property and the assets are ours free and clear.

THE SUPERIOR DISTRICT COURT FOR THE STATE OF ALASKA and its Officer Michelle Boutin failed to honor its own published "law" and continued its assault against us and against our ESTATE property.

That we are separate, civilian, and Third Parties not owned as chattel by the United States of America, Incorporated, not standing as sureties thereof, and not made debtors merely because of fraud practiced upon us was clearly established by our actions presenting the ESTATE "Birth Certificates" to THE SUPERIOR DISTRICT COURT FOR THE STATE OF ALASKA.

The Birth Certificates are monetized securities presented to the COURT for redemption by the actual beneficiaries of these "ESTATES" and are proof that (1) the NAMES thereon are **not** the same as the name of the trust that the property discussed in the foreclosure action is held under; (2) that the estates of the "decedants" listed were probated improperly and under false presumptions resulting in the improper hypothecation of debt against the ESTATES; (3) that we, living Americans, are the actual beneficiaries of these Puerto Rican ESTATE trusts, and that we are the equitable title holders of all the ESTATE assets, including the monthly mortgage payments that we paid in error and which are **owed to us**; (4) the ESTATES established and monetized "in our names" are Roman Inferior Trusts — as beneficiaries reclaiming our controlling interest in these ESTATES, we are owed return of all assets free and clear of debt hypothecated against our assets by any and all secondary beneficiaries — including the United States of America, Inc., including the UNITED STATES, INC., including any and all debts of their franchises and agencies and corporations organized under their auspices.

Attack upon our private trust d.b.a. "Anna M. Riezinger-von Reitz and James C. Belcher" is an attack against the trust property interests of American civilians who are Third Parties being harmed and defrauded as a result of improper trust administration and claims resulting from constructive fraud practiced by the officers of the United States of America, Inc. and the forced imposition of "Federal Reserve Notes" as legal tender under conditions of monopoly inducement and in breach of trust and contract.

Under international law, including the international Law of the Sea, the action of THE SUPERIOR DISTRICT COURT FOR THE STATE OF ALASKA and its officer, Michelle Boutin, against our private trust and their pretended jurisdiction over our redeemed trust assets in general, is both constructive fraud and a war crime for which the United States of America (Minor) and the United Nations stand responsible.

To give the non-lawyers an insight into the situation:

The United States of America, Inc. acting in Breach of Trust and without granted consent, created *foreign situs* trusts which it operated under our names styled in Upper and Lower case letters: e.g., John Quincy Adams. This corporation and its officers who were under contract to defend our national trust and provide governmental services to our organic states then claimed that these *foreign situs* trusts were standing as "surety" for their own private corporate debts — circumstantially implying that individual living Americans had voluntarily agreed to stand good for the debts of the United States of America, Inc. and that they and their property and the assets of their organic states were all valid collateral for the debts of the privately owned and operated United States of America, Inc.

This was done without granted authority, without disclosure, and without consent by officers of a privately owned and operated corporation merely under contract to provide enumerated services to the victims.

It was and is pure, self-interested fraud based on semantic deceits, and it was carried out without disclosure as a "private" matter concerning only the United States of America, Incorporated and its officers — not the clearly intended victims of the constructive fraud.

None of the corporate officers engaging in this activity and making these absurd claims upon the actual **employers** of the United States of America, Inc. had any granted authority to make these representations "in behalf" of anyone, much less the people they were bound to serve.

The United States of America, Inc. was entered into receivership. The Trustee of the bankruptcy, the Secretary of the Treasury of Puerto Rico, promptly created new "public trusts" under the NAMES of the individual living Americans, e.g., JOHN QUINCY ADAMS, within the jurisdiction of the United States of America (Minor), and "removed" the original *foreign situs* trusts together with their assets to Puerto Rican jurisdiction.

You and everything you own have (supposedly) come under the jurisdiction of Puerto Rico and the corporate United States. The problem with this is that it has all been accomplished on the basis of non-disclosure and fraud and fraud vitiates — that is, utterly destroys and negates — everything it aims to accomplish.

So there is and can be no valid claim raised by any of these incorporated entities, nor by their bill collectors, against you or your estate. As the FINAL NOTICE clearly stated, this **fact** has already been **determined and decided** at the very highest levels of world governance and by the Trustee of the Global Estate Trust, the Pope, who has demanded compliance from the corporate United States and all its various corporate franchises and agencies — including the State of Alaska and the STATE OF ALASKA and from the United Nations operating the UNITED STATES and its franchise the STATE OF ALASKA and so on.

All the fraud, all the false claims being made against American ESTATES, has to come to an end.

What remains to be done, and what has been done in the demonstration cases, is to redeem the individual ESTATES — that is, to reclaim and restore these ESTATES and their assets to their natural beneficiaries, free and clear of all encumbrances created by fraud and by mis-administration by incompetent or criminally inclined trustees.

The proof of everything said here is evident on the face of the Birth Certificates provided by the various agencies responsible for administering this massive international fraud.

The Birth Certificate documents are all securitized and monetized — bonded, in fact, and issued on bond paper and traded on exchanges — in the NAME of Puerto Rican ESTATE trusts, as a result of **probate** proceedings and are clearly signed by **Registrars** — officers of the various local probate courts. These ESTATES are all Roman Inferior Trusts.

What does this mean?

JOHN QUINCY ADAMS (insert your NAME) is an ESTATE trust whose actual beneficiary is "presumed dead".

You, the living man or woman, born as an American on the land of one of the organic American states are the "missing" beneficiary, though you must hack through two layers of fraud to establish the fact and kick the butt of the American Bar Association all the way to Puerto Rico.

You, the living man or woman, are in precisely the same situation as Robinson Crusoe returning home after being away for twenty years. Robinson's estate has been seized by the courts, probated, rolled over into a Roman Inferior Estate Trust — also known as a Cestui Que Vie Trust — and handed over to his butler. The butler has had a wild time, charged up Robinson's credit cards, mortgaged his estate, invested and spent his money, drunk up the wine cellar, and caused the Crusoe name to fall into disrepute. Now, at long last, Robinson has returned and presented irrefutable proof of his identity and his status as a living man owed the return of his property free and clear of all the debts and encumbrances placed upon it as a result of misadministration, fraud, and fiduciary malfeasance on the part of his (former) butler. In addition, in this case, "Robinson" is owed reparations from the court for failure to immediately return his property to his control and void all claims established since the improper probate of his estate, and also from the corporation administering the

"government" for failure to impose oversight on the probate court which colluded with the butler and gave the estate assets to the butler instead of to the rightful heirs.

That's where you are now if you are an American born on the land of one of the organic states of the Union — and it is all the result of breach of trust, gross fiduciary malfeasance, unlawful conversion, semantic deceit and non-disclosure — and other criminal activities undertaken by two foreign corporations merely hired under commercial contract to protect you and your assets and to provide nineteen enumerated governmental services. It has been further exacerbated by ignorant and corrupt state legislators who have colluded with the erring federal government officials.

The FEDERAL RESERVE, operating as a "new" corporation formed under the auspices of the United Nations (which is a separate international city-state), is pretending that it owns you as a slave and owns your ESTATE assets, too. It is pretending that it, not we, have controlling interest in our ESTATE assets, and even though its claims are clearly rebutted and disproven as a self-serving fiction, it is continuing to prosecute marine salvage liens under "Special Admiralty" rules created by these perpetrators to expedite this fraud against Americans.

This unlawful prosecution is continuing even though we have presented the "certificates" issued by the probate court to form our "ESTATES" under the false presumption of our death and by presenting these to the COURT and properly identifying ourselves, we have in fact "redeemed" our ESTATES and placed them back in their original jurisdiction and under our private control.

We have objected to the fraud and to the strong-arm extortion that the FEDERAL RESERVE and its agencies d.b.a. the ALASKA COURT SYSTEM, INC. and THE SUPERIOR DISTRICT COURT FOR THE STATE OF ALASKA have engaged in against us, and we are holding the STATE OF

ALASKA as the local franchise of the UNITED STATES, INC. — the Trustee — responsible for failing to take action in our behalf and failure to exercise administrative control over corporations that have been formed under UNITED STATES auspices and which are operating in a criminal fashion against the peaceful inhabitants of the land.

There either is or is not a contract.

These corporations are operating in violation of their charters and are subject to dissolution as criminal enterprises. We have demanded immediate correction and to date, they have not self-corrected nor has the STATE OF ALASKA taken the necessary action as the local franchise operator to impose correction. The GOVERNOR and ATTORNEY GENERAL are culpable in the extreme for this circumstance and also responsible for the continuing false arrest of Alaskans James L. Jensen, Jr. and Robin L. Jensen.

In their most recent and audacious move yet, THE SUPERIOR COURT FOR THE STATE OF ALASKA, yet another "COURT" separate and distinct from "THE SUPERIOR DISTRICT COURT FOR THE STATE OF ALASKA" has "ordered" the "execution sale" of property and assets belonging to us that are **not** mortgaged and **not** under any valid contract whatsoever with **any** entity created by, belonging to, or administered by these charlatans or the banks that operate them, properties which have already been formally released from any "federal lien" whatsoever. They and their officer, Michelle Boutin, have advertised a "JUDICIAL FORECLOSURE SALE" in the absence of any "judicial" power whatsoever.

Every member of the law enforcement agencies and the military commanders are on Notice of this circumstance, from the Provost Marshals to the U.S.marshals Office, to the FBI to the Alaska State Troopers. So is Interpol. And so is the Pope.

The same exact circumstances and conditions apply to the misadministration of the ESTATES of 390 million Americans, and it must be resolved in their favor.

Meanwhile it is important for everyone involved to understand that the "government" is just another corporation under contract to provide specified services for hire, that this problem is not limited to America, and that the real civil government resides in the individual living Americans who have **unlimited civil power** on the land of the organic states.

All of the crimes, frauds, and failures described herein have taken place *outside* the land jurisdiction of The United States of America, in "international waters" — but it hardly matters, because fraud is fraud upon the sea as upon the land, and fraud vitiates all claims based upon it.

On May 28, 2014, officers of THE SUPERIOR COURT FOR THE STATE OF ALASKA are advertising a "JUDICIAL FORECLOSURE SALE" of some of our **redeemed** ESTATE property under the patently self-serving and continuing false presumption that we, living Americans, and our **redeemed** ESTATES, are sureties for the debts of the United States of America, Inc. and are responsible for the expenses of its BANKRUPTCY TRUSTEES, including their expenses to prosecute our ESTATES under these false presumptions in the TRUSTEE'S own private COURTS.

However, this fraud has been fully recognized by the **Global Estate Trust**.

We are the priority creditors of the bankrupt United States of America, Inc. We are their employers and creditors, not their employees and not their debtors in this situation.

The men engaging in these acts of mis-administration are criminals who have worked a complex, highly coercive, multigenerational fraud scheme known as a "Reverse Trust Scheme" against us, against every other American born on the land, and against many other national governments as well.

If the international banks and the members of the BAR Associations do not come into compliance with the actual law and respect the property rights of Americans, Canadians, and others who have been impacted by similar "public trust" schemes, their corporations will be dissolved and their professional associations will be outlawed and disbanded. Individual bankers and lawyers who have knowingly and willingly participated in this fraud will be branded as criminals, their property will be confiscated, and they will be deported from The United States of America.

It's really that simple and just a matter of time before everyone knows what has gone on here, who did it, who is responsible for this deplorable criminality, and why. Those responsible would do well to take *immediate* determined actions to correct.

21. Are the accompanying "Civil Orders" legitimate? Do I have to act upon them as an elected, appointed, or commissioned officer?

Yes, you do. Remember that every living American born on the soil of one of the fifty states United is literally an internationally recognized sovereign on the land of those states. In administering our affairs and those of our organic states, our will is absolute. These Civil Orders are issued under civil, commercial, and canon authority **without representation**. The Constitution for the united States of America, the Treaty of Paris, the applicable Treaties of Westminster, and the Treaty of Ghent, which establish and protect the national trust of The United States of America and our individual estates must be honored.

American states operating in sovereign original jurisdiction have issued these Civil Orders commanding compliance from the (E)STATE trustees, administrators, and employees, requiring their proper performance under contract. **There is no higher authority.**

To reduce it to practical terms — when you accept a job you are obligated to perform your duties. Wouldn't you expect to be fired, if you didn't? Are you obligated to obey your actual employer, the owner of the company? Or do you think you will fare better obeying a middle-manager who is giving you opposing orders and merely claiming to "represent" the boss? Don't you have to perform on your contracts?

We think it is obvious that you are obligated to obey your actual employers, not those who merely claim to represent them. No amount of corruption, criminality, or fraud serves to obscure the claim of Americans on American private property, and American states.

This is both a public and a private matter, and has been made so by acts of fraud and violence perpetuated by corporations acting in violation of their charters as criminal enterprises, all of which have been operated in maritime and admiralty jurisdictions in breach of trust.

22. <u>Are you telling me that changing from an unincorporated government to an incorporated government is like an evil twin brother usurping an estate from a rightful heir?</u>

Not quite. The United States of America has no twin, but it does have a tumor-like foreign outgrowth which has turned parasitic and which is transgressing against the Body Politic.

In commercial terms — when people act **as** people they come together in free association and act under full commercial liability. They are responsible and accountable for their debts and deeds. When people form corporations to "represent" them or their interests in some capacity, and bring these corporations together in association, what you get is a corporate conglomerate that is **not** fully accountable for its debts and deeds because of the corporate veil. This "veil" is the same veil that stands between life and death.

Incorporated "persons" — which include commercial corporations, trusts, cooperatives, trusts, and foundations — are considered dead. They have no motive force of their own. They are operated by third parties under charters granted by nations and states that have themselves all been chartered by the Holy See. Such entities have a natural limited liability, because they are not conscious. When such entities are formed, the intentions and purposes of their creators are clearly stated and typically include a catch-all phrase — "any other lawful purpose" — to cover additional unforeseen circumstances. All corporations are required to function lawfully and in accord with their charters. Any violation of their charter, such as deviation from their stated purpose or failure to perform it, any unlawful activity whatsoever, provides grounds to demand dissolution of a corporate entity and distribution of its assets to its creditors.

Because corporations are not fully liable for "their" acts, they are allowed to go bankrupt without prejudice against their owners and operators. Only assets belonging to the corporation are subject to bankruptcy. The privately held assets of the owners and operators are not affected.

Thus, when the United States of America, Incorporated, went bankrupt in 1933, its President, Franklin Delano Roosevelt, was not bankrupted and neither were the members of the "US Congress" running it as corporate officers. The organic states and the American people should never have been subject to its bankruptcy, either, and wouldn't have been, except that the Roosevelt Administration falsely and deliberately claimed that they were "voluntary" assets standing as surety for the debts of the United States of America, Inc.

This claim was based on a "pledge" made by the Conference of Governors acting on March 6, 1933. These "Governors" — men operating "State" franchises of the United States of America, Inc. — gratuitously promised the "good faith and credit of their states and the citizenry thereof" without bothering to explicitly say which or what kind of "state" or "citizenry" they were referring to when they made this pledge. Everyone present presumably knew that their public office did not grant them any ability to promise resources belonging to the American states much less the private property of the American People, but the creditors gleefully presumed that the organic states and the American people were legitimately on the hook, extended vast amounts of credit to the perpetrators, and began advancing false claims against the resources of the organic states and the private property of the American People.

Imagine that Burger King, International, went bankrupt, called a meeting of all the local franchise owners, and asked them to pledge the assets **of their customers** as collateral backing the debts of Burger King, International.

That's what happened in 1933.

There's just one real monkey wrench in this for the perpetrators and their central bank buddies. **It's all fraud and fraud vitiates everything it touches.** The "Governors" had no legitimate authority to pledge even a square foot of American soil, much less pledge the private property assets of the American People. That they purported to do this and that the self-interested bankers and lawyers allowed them to do this, is an act of criminality that staggers the imagination.

It is identity theft, impersonation of public officials, semantic deceit, unlawful conversion, and constructive fraud carried out on a planetary basis. Not only were the American People and their organic states cruelly victimized, so were their friends and neighbors and trading partners. Meanwhile, the members of the

"US Congress" changed hats to become members of the "US CONGRESS", and, glutting on the vast amounts of credit being offered to them — all based on their patently false claim that they had granted authority to sell everything and everyone in America as chattel and to use us and our land as surety for their private corporate debts — they charged up our credit cards to the hilt and left us to pay the bill.

That is why the "US government" needs to be entirely reformed, the reason that every member of "CONGRESS" and every "GOVERNOR" and every member of every "STATE LEGISLATURE" needs to be jack-booted in the rump, the reason that the assets of all the complicit banks need to be confiscated, the reason that the current banking institutions and their supposed "watch dog agencies" like the SEC need to be dissolved as criminal enterprises, the reason that all "national debt" needs to be repudiated worldwide, the reason that the Bar Associations — worldwide — need to be disbanded and outlawed, the reason that the "City State" status of the District of Columbia and the United Nations — both — needs to be rescinded, the reason that the English People likewise need to rescind the "City State" status of the Inner City of London and flush Fleet Street and the Crown Temple into the Thames.

The immense power of the Pope's Temporal Office needs to be employed to straighten out this steaming manure pile of government "service" organizations once and for all.

How are we going to accomplish this? Simple. We tell each other the truth, we forgive each other, we liquidate the offending corporations, we prosecute those who have purposefully and knowingly perpetuated this fraud, and we start over with a clean slate. The People of Iceland have already done this successfully. There is no reason that the rest of the world can't do the same.

As for the American People it is long overdue for us to dust off our laurels and walk the walk as true world leaders, instead of allowing ourselves to be directed by thugs, and letting criminals set up shop in our banks, courthouses, and seats of government. A housecleaning of major proportions is long overdue, and the image of "Rosie, the Riveter" comes to mind.

The perpetrators of this fraud will want to defend themselves and continue making their false claims and continue bilking the American People. They will make all sorts of threats and accusations and try to start trouble, maybe even try to make the American Armed Services and other "government agencies" use force against the People of the Land. If they do so, they will only identify themselves as criminals and make their status as criminals crystal clear for the entire world to see.

23. <u>There are really only 22 questions, but this one answers the dreadful unasked moral question.</u>

Pity Pope Francis, the man who has inherited this incredible convoluted and criminal mess. He is doing his best to straighten it out, but he needs help — your help. If you are an American and the least bit interested in your own future and the false claims being made against your property assets and those of your organic states, it is time to take affirmative, positive, determined, and non-violent action.

Pope Francis is being attacked, viciously, by hired media and propaganda masters who are working hard every day at the behest of the banks and the Bar Associations to vilify the Roman Catholic Church — which is now the primary obstacle in the way of achieving — not a gentle, kind, unified government for the world that respects free will and individual people as Children of God — but a demonic version sponsored by the Crown Temple.

These two organizations are rivals by design. The Roman Catholic Church worships God, the Creator. The Crown Temple worships Lucifer, the Liar. In past ages these organizations have engaged as necessary evils endemic to creation, each one bent on

137

corrupting the other in an endless cycle — one drawing good out of evil, and the other dedicated to creating evil out of good.

This reflects the duality seen everywhere and in everyone.

The Church stands in bright light, in robes of white, advocating life. The Crown Temple stands in the darkness, wears robes of black, and advocates death.

It is no coincidence that the followers of Lucifer indulge in such a fantastic array of semantic deceits, false identities, corporate personas, and lies, for they literally worship the Father of All Lies. It is no mistake that they seize by deceit and violence and lay waste to human lives, because they worship Satan. This is not really any secret. They have existed and endeavored to rule over everyone else since 3760 BC. They were insane then and they are insane now. In Babylon, their priests self-castrated and practiced every possible kind of violence and black magic. They murdered (by burning alive) infants in the name of their goddess. All that has changed is that in modern times cult members keep their working parts, and worship a male deity instead. They still defend mass murder of infants. They still deal in illusions — legal **fiction** entities and fiat money. They still wear black robes.

Which side will win the eternal battle?

Pope Francis is standing firm for all that is right and real, for life, for love, for justice, for truth. Those in charge of the Crown Temple are standing just as firm for evil, for death, for hatred, for injustice, for lies. At any time, the Pope could falter and become the Anti-Christ. At any time, the Anti-Christ could fail and be relinquished to the dustbin of history.

The great dream of the Church is the Kingdom of God on earth, a peaceful kingdom built on life and love. The great dream of the Crown Temple is to rule, period, forever, as the slave master of others. Just as "the corporate United States" pretends to be The United States of America, the Crown Temple often pretends to be the Roman Catholic Church. Sometimes, quite often, they succeed in planting their operatives in the Church.

That's why the Church gets branded with all the infamy and violence that results when one of the Crown Temple members gains prominence. Crown Temple initiates brought us the Inquisition and similar atrocities — all "in the name of" and wearing the vestments of the Roman Catholic Church. This is why the Church has been bedecked with gold and jewels and treasures, surrounded by Egyptian obelisks and other fertility symbols — not to reflect a love of God, but to glorify a perverse worship of sexuality, not to adorn the Church, but to silently coerce and implicate and tempt and deceive and enslave and provide excuse to accuse the Roman Catholic Church of all the sins of the Crown Temple. To this day, all priests of Satan must first gain priesthood in the Roman Catholic Church: if you are dedicated and duplicitous enough to be ordained as a Roman Catholic priest while secretly worshiping Lucifer, you have passed your entry level test as a Satanist.

Apologists have tried to excuse the existence of the Crown Temple as a necessary evil built into the fabric of the natural world. They postulate that without its lies and fake money and the violence and conflict it perpetuates every day, people would have nothing to motivate them and the world's economy would collapse. People are livestock, they say, here merely to exist for our profit, to be milked, shorn, and slaughtered. If people were allowed to use and enjoy the resources that properly belong to them, they'd sit on their rumps all day and drink pina coladas (like we do) and all the processes and work necessary for our comfort and profit would grind to a halt.

Others have taken the stance that continuing to tolerate the Crown Temple in our midst is like allowing a giant colony of disease-infested rats, or a cancer, to consume the globe. The underlying insanity of the Masters of Deceit is all too apparent to justify allowing them to continue their rampages. They brought us both the First and Second World Wars without a thought or backward glance. During their hegemony in America, they have kept the American people constantly embroiled in wars for profit throughout the globe, which has caused Americans to be hated and feared by decent and innocent people everywhere. They have done this at the same time that they have bilked the American "taxpayers" for credit that supposedly supports welfare recipients and foreign aid — but which is actually siphoned off to benefit the criminals and fund their operations among us.

Less than 20% of all money supposedly appropriated for welfare payments and less than 2% of foreign aid ever reaches its purported destinations.

Nothing is what it seems. The courts are the criminals. The "money" is worthless debt. The gods are the servants. The students are the teachers. Everything on earth is upside down and reversed. Everything that you think is separate is in fact unified and everything that you think is wrong is ultimately right.

Perhaps most important — everything that you think is secret is fully known.

Those who describe their brothers and sisters as "useless eaters" and who strive to defraud and control and pillage and rape and murder for profit and pleasure, and also those who refuse to forgive and refuse to provide justice — take note — **there are no secrets**. From that enlightened perspective, you will finally see the very real need to reform your precious Self.

All those who cherish what is good in their hearts, who know their weakness, who are able to feel love and gratitude, who yearn for justice, who sigh and moan every day for relief — all your deeds, motives, and circumstances, even the inmost desires of your hearts are also known.

So it is written: what is done in secret will be declared from the housetops, and the truth shall set men free.

The truth will inevitably invade your mind like a virus download onto a computer. You will realize that nobody can represent you and that "representative government" is a ridiculous lie. You will require government to be your servant, not a ruler over you. You will know that you belong to the land, but that the land does not belong to you. You will know that lines drawn on a map are just lines on a map. You will see the illusion within which you have lived, and you will realize your guilt in the same breath you behold your victimhood.

You can be a shepherd or you can be a wolf, but you no longer can be a sheep.

The great sin for which the Americans are responsible does not digest the world in the bowels of London, but roams on the Great Plains of America and throughout the 50 states United. It is in the hearts and minds and lives of the American Indians we have defrauded and attacked, reducing them to abject poverty and alienation via cultural actual genocide.

The American Indians have suffered terribly because they know and hold onto this one simple truth: we do not own land.

Nobody does.

The land owns us.

Like every other lie and illusion practiced by the Crown Temple, Europeans became infected early on with the idea that men could own land, and based upon this central lie, a vast complex of other lies has been built.

The followers of the Crown Temple have created, engendered, and promoted this insanity as a means to control others and provide endless excuses for conflict — which creates profit for themselves at everyone else's expense. The idea of "incorporation" is similarly immoral, insane, and destructive. Commercial corporations exist for one reason only — to escape accountability. On this basis alone their existence should be outlawed. The Great Lie of representative government is another chestnut created by the Crown Temple, a blatant impossibility that has been enshrined without question for over two hundred years.

When the Americans declared that all men are equal, they meant it. There is no basis for the empowerment of one equal over another *equal*. Likewise when they declared their determination to enjoy free speech, free travel, and other rights of Nature, there was no room left for the egotism of rebellious public servants. Under American law and under the American government there is no power greater than each individual. This means that we cannot be represented and although we may transgress and may even be outlawed, we cannot be harassed, subjected, nor demeaned as a "thing" — such as an ESTATE or a *foreign situs* trust or a transmitting utility.

The Final Judgment and accompanying Civil Orders have been signed and sealed and now also this information is being sealed under the authority of **anu:hotep** giving voice, sign, and seal, proving that those who know the Lie also know the Truth.

6
Primary Source Documents

1. Treaties with St. Boniface and Treaties Between the Holy See and King Pepin the Short of the Franks; Pepin delivered and defended the Papal states of the Holy See, confirming the "temporal powers" of Rome and laying the groundwork for his son, Charlemagne, to create the First Holy Roman Empire. (751-800 A.D.)

2. Charter of the First Holy Roman Empire, 800 A.D.

3. King John of England breaks with the Roman Catholic Church, 1209. Edict of Excommunication of John of England.

4. Treaty of King John of England, Cede to Innocent III, 1213 A.D. John agrees that England and Ireland are both "fiefs" of Rome, and that his own crown will be forfeited to Rome if he breaks his sworn agreements favoring the Pope.

5. Magna Carta 1215 A.D. In signing the Magna Carta King John silently invoked the 1213 Papal agreement relinquishing his crown to the Pope. Thereafter, all lands explored and claimed in behalf of Catholic Monarchs, **including the British Monarch as a vassal of Rome**, were in fact first and wholly claimed in behalf of the Holy See, which returned a portion of the profit to the vassal monarchs in the form of "jurisdictions". The Holy See retained the global jurisdiction of the air, granted jurisdiction of the land to temporal authorities (recognized monarchs), and granted the international jurisdiction of the sea to the British Crown Temple to be administered under the ancient Law of the Sea (international admiralty) and Law Merchant (now Uniform Commercial Code).

6. Charter(s) of the **Global Estate Trust** (1455, 1456, 1479, and 1492 et alia) by Papal Bulls, especially the Inter Ceatera of May 3 and 4, 1493, by Pope Alexander VI.

7. European Treaties bearing on the History of the United States and its Dependencies to 1648. — Frances Gardiner Davenport, editor, Carnegie Institution of Washington, 1917, Washington, D.C., especially pp. 75-78.

8. "The Privileges and Prerogatives Granted by Their Catholic Majesties to Christopher Columbus April 30, 1492"

9. "The First Charter of Virginia" April 10, 1606

10. "The Second Charter of Virginia" 23 May 1609

11. "The Third Charter of Virginia" March 12, 1611

12. "The Charter of New England: 1620" It becomes obvious from the above that all these E(states) were formed as commercial ventures under the auspices of Monarchies owing fealty to the Holy See.

13. "Cestui Que Vie Act of 1666" — Sets forth the nature and construction of Roman Inferior Trusts in England to allow state management of property belonging of unknown survivors of the Black Death and the Fire of London.

14. "Charter for the Province of Pennsylvania — 1681" — More proof of the commercial and non-religious nature of the founding principles that the Holy See employs in managing its temporal affairs and providing governmental services.

15. "Charter of the Corporation of the Bank of England 1694"

16. The Articles of Confederation 1781

17. The Treaty(ies) of Paris plus Amends, 1784-90

18. The Treaty of Westminster, 1794, a "Treaty of Amity, Commerce, and Navigation" between HIS BRITANNIC MAJESTY AND THE UNITED STATES OF AMERICA, November 19, 1794, in which the British Crown commercial company and its American version agreed to peace in perpetuity.

19. The Northwest Ordinance, 1787.

20. The Constitution for the united States of America, 1789.

21. Act of February 20, 1792, Establishing a General Post Office for the United States government, in addition to the already existing general post office.

22. 1818: U.S. v. Bevans, 16 U.S.336. Establishes two separate jurisdictions within the United States Of America: 1. The "federal zone" and 2. "the 50 States".

23. The Treaty of Ghent, 1814

24. Treaty of Verona, 1822, American Diplomatic Code, 1778 - 1884, vol. 2 ; Elliott, p. 179 and CONGRESSIONAL RECORD - SENATE.,64th CONGRESS, 1st SESSION, VOLUME 53, PART 7, Page 6781, 25 April 1916, in which the Higher Contracting Powers agreed to undermine the American government.

25. "Bankruptcy Law (of England)" 1826

26. "First Bank Act (America)" 1863

27. **The Lieber Code** also known as General Order 100, April 24, 1863, by President Abraham Lincoln as Commander in Chief, making the Union Army responsible for proper administration of the monetary system, protection of the National Trust, and fair treatment of the Southern States and their inhabitants during reconstruction. **The Lieber Code requires the Army, or in modern terms, the Department of Defense, to pay reparations to all non-combatant civilians harmed.** This Code

has never been repealed or changed. It is the reason that we continue to have "Secretary **Generals**" and "US Postmaster **Generals**" and "Attorney **Generals**" and "Inspector **Generals**" and "**Lieutenant** Governors".

28. The Reform Act of 1867 (Britain) — First use of **enfranchisement** as a political tool **to undermine legal standing** of living men under Chancellor of the Exchequer, Benjamin Disraeli.

29. The Reconstruction Act of 1867 – American counterpart

30. "the Constitution of the United States of America" 1871 – established by the "US Congress" acting as Board of Directors to form the **United States of America, Inc.** as a Trust Management Organization to operate both the municipal government of **the to come corporate United States** and to administer and fulfill the National Trust Indenture and service contracts owed the now-50 states known as **The United States of America**.

31. The Act of 1871 – Formally incorporated the municipal (city state) government of the District of Columbia as a separate nation operated according to its own government and code.

32. ***Merriam's Estate,*** 36 NE 505, 506 22: "... the United States is to be regarded as a body politic and corporate. ... It is suggested that the United States is to be regarded as a **domestic corporation,** so far as the State of New York is concerned. We think this contention has no support in reason or authority. ... The United States is a **foreign corporation** in relation to a State."

33. ***U.S. v. Anthony,*** 24 Fed. 829 (1873) "The term resident and **citizen of the United States** is distinguished from a Citizen of one of the several states, in that the former is **a special class of citizen created by Congress**." Though the judge fails to fully admit the circumstance, "US citizenship" was created as an excuse for the "government" to claim ownership of all the slaves supposedly freed by the Civil War as chattel backing Union war

debts. To this day, black Americans have only "Civil Rights".

34. ***U.S. v. Cruikshank,*** 92 U.S. 542, 23 L.Ed. 588, (1875). "There is in our political system [two governments], a government of the Several [50] States, and a government of the United States. Each is distinct from the other and has citizens of its own. A person may be a citizen of the United States and of a State, and as such has different rights."

35. ***United States v. Germane,*** 99 U.S. 508 (1879), ***Norton v. Shelby County,*** 118 U.S. 425, 441, 6 S.Ct. 1121 (1866), etc., dating to ***Pope v. Commissioner,*** 138 F.2d 1006, 1009 (6th Cir. 1943); where the state is concerned, the most recent corresponding decision was ***State v. Pinckney,*** 276 N.W.2d 433,436 (Iowa 1979). All these are supporting case law establishing ***res judicata*** regarding the nature of The United States (original TMO) and a State (one of "Several States" of the Union) as first expressed in the ***Merriam's Estate*** case cited above.

36. Title 8 USC §§ 1101(a), (3), (21) and (22) and Public Law, 15 U.S. Stat., Chapter 249, pps 223-224. Under Federal Code (the internal "law" of the United States of America, Inc.) there is no such thing as dual citizenship.

37. Title 8 USC 1101(a)(21) the birthright status of **"American Nationals"** is recognized. Under the statutory law of the United States of America, Inc. there is absolute distinction between **"US citizens"** and **"American Nationals"**.

38. **The Clearfield Doctrine** and USC Title 22: When a government operates as a commercial corporation it descends to the level of all such corporations and has no special powers or attributes. It is only when acting as a properly formed unincorporated Body Politic that a government exercises sovereign power of any kind. **Virtually all governments operating in the world today are for-profit corporations under contract to provide governmental services.** The American "US

(Major)" government (The United States of America) hasn't operated as a sovereign entity since 1865. The US (Minor) government (the corporate United States) operates as a corporation.

39. *The Insular Tariff Cases,* US Supreme Court, 1900-1904 – A series of US Supreme Court cases that resulted in allowing Congress to operate "the corporate United States" — DC, Guam, Puerto Rico, et alia — as a separate and foreign nation state **without regard for the requirements imposed by** The Constitution for the united States of America. From one of the cases, *Downes v. Bidwell,* 182 U.S. 244 (1901), we quote Justice Marshall Harlan writing in dissent: "...two national governments, one to be maintained under the Constitution, with all its restrictions, the other to be maintained by Congress outside and independently of that instrument, by exercising such powers as other nations of the earth are accustomed to...a radical and mischievous change in our system of government will result...We will, in that event, *pass from the era of constitutional liberty guarded and protected by a written constitution into an era of legislative absolutism*...It will be an evil day for American liberty if the theory of a government outside the supreme law of the land finds lodgment in our constitutional jurisprudence."

40. Charter of The Corporation Trust Company of America, 1907 A.D.

41. *Hendrick v. Maryland S.C. Reporter's Rd.,* 610-625. (1914) "A "US Citizen" upon leaving the District of Columbia becomes involved in "interstate commerce", *as a "resident" does not have the common-law right to travel of a Citizen of one of the several states*." This "power of the Congress" to rule over the people of the District of Columbia and the Insular states was used as an excuse *to impose Driver Licenses* on "US citizens" living *outside* the confines of the United States of America and mis-applied to Citizens of the corporate United States — so-

called "State Citizens" who were entrapped into contract by a process of mis-administration and legal presumption. This applies to the myriad **"licenses"** and **"codes"** that have been mis-applied to the American People under undisclosed, misrepresented, and otherwise invalid private contracts.

42. The Federal Reserve Act, 1913. Allows a private non-federal for-profit banking association doing business under the purposefully deceitful name of "Federal Reserve" to commandeer the national monetary and economic systems, allowing these banks to print money and back only a small "fractional" portion of it with gold or silver. Later, they will be allowed to back the money with nothing at all but the promises of the US Congress.

43. Trading With the Enemy Act, Public Law No. 65-91 (40 Stat. L. 411) October 6, 1917, defines non-combatant American civilian Nationals and their States as "enemies" of the corporate United States. This Act originally *excluded* citizens of the United States, but in the Act of March 9, 1933, Section 2 amended this to *included* "any person within the United States or any place subject to the jurisdiction thereof". This has been used as a self-serving and transparent *excuse* to commit fraud and violence against Americans who never recognized any such "state of war" between themselves or their States and the corporate United States and who were instead already owed full fiduciary care under *commercial equity contract* (The Constitution for the united States of America), *reparations* under the Lieber Code, and *trusteeship* from the **Global Estate Trust**.

44. The Maternity Act /The Sheppard-Towner Act, 1921, first foray into socialized medicine and "registration" of live births.

45. Minutes of the Geneva Convention(s), May 1930. Declare international bankruptcy via treaties between the G5 nations. The United States of America, Inc. was bankrupted internationally along with the Trust Management Organizations of four European nations including Great Britain, which caused the

domino effect of bankruptcy worldwide. Note that the real property assets held by each national trust — land, vegetation, animals, natural resources, etc. — are held in **perpetual trust** and are required to be unaffected by the ups and downs of any Trust Management Organization charged as Trustees to administer business affairs in behalf of the beneficiaries, who are the living people who inhabit the land of each country and continent.

46. Amended Charter renaming the above as The Corporation Trust Company, April 15, 1930.

47. Executive Order 6073 issued on March 10, 1933, created the "bank holiday" and closed the doors of the bankrupt government chartered banks (they were bankrupted as a whole because they operated under government charter, and because of the Great Fraud committed by the Governors of the several States, **not because they were individually bankrupt**).

48. Executive Order 6102 issued on April 5, 1933, prohibited "hoarding" gold and required people to turn it (their private property) in to the Federal Reserve Banks (the creditors) under the false and undisclosed presumption that they were volunteering to stand as sureties for the debts of the United States of America, Inc.

49. Executive Order 6111 issued on April 20, 1933, prohibited people from exporting gold.

The creditors (banks) claimed that all the gold in private hands in the Several (now 50) States no longer belonged to the State Citizens and other Inhabitants, as a result of having been pledged to the State by corporate officers of the privately owned and operated United States of America, Inc., acting as deceitfully named State "Governors", so confiscation of privately held American gold resources was instituted under conditions of false pretense and semantic deceit by officers of a bankrupted privately owned and operated Trust Management Organization and their creditors, privately owned and operated international banks —
150

the World Bank (now IMF), IBRD, and Federal Reserve.

COMMERCIAL REMEDY

H.J. Res 192, 73rd Congress, First Session, principally prior enrolled as Public Law, U.S. Statutes at Large, Vol. 1, Public Acts, 3rd Congress, 2nd Session, Chapter 48, especially 48.48.112 —This is the commercial remedy that the perpetrators were required to create *to make their confiscation* of private gold and hypothecated titles to private land and business holdings *"legal". This remedy* like the underlying surreptitious hypothecation of debt and claims against private property made by the officers of the United States of America, Inc. against the American Nationals *was never widely circulated or disclosed* for obvious reasons. Unaware of how they'd been injured and abused by those obligated to act as their Trustees, the inhabitants of the land were equally unable to access *this remedy,* which *was for the government corporation to literally <u>pre-pay</u> all debts owed by the foreign situs trusts* created to stand as sureties of the United States of America, Inc. Like irresponsible teenagers promising to make the payments on a car, the US Congress "resolved" to pay its debts in such a way *that the presumed co-signers on US Congress loans, the foreign situs trusts* they named after American Nationals — *would never default,* and in theory, the living American Nationals would never be dunned or otherwise impacted by their fraudulent semantic deceits and false claims.

In actual practice, *the voucher and coupon system* which should have been ubiquitously implemented never was, and the Internal Revenue Service, the agency responsible *for collecting taxes and dispensing credit* owed to individual accounts was split into two distinct and separate entities, **the Internal Revenue Service operated by the Federal Reserve** *for collecting taxes,* and the **IRS operated by the International Monetary Fund** *for dispensing credit,* which colluded to confuse and defraud the living people, billing them "as if" they owed the tax bills and forcing them to pay the debts of the make-believe *foreign situs* trusts operated under their names using Federal Reserve Notes, a process that not only failed to pay the debts of these "fictional citizens" of the corporate United States but left the American Nationals even further in debt as a result of interest and service fees and import duties charged by the same banks.

50. U.S. Bankruptcy Act of 1933, especially Section 101 (11) — Declares the American People as the Creditors, and the "United States" as the Obligator, or Debtor. This established that *the signatures of Americans are to be used as credit, and the "State" franchises of the United States of America, Inc,* d.b.a. "United States", "State of Ohio", etc., and their Trustees, d.b.a. Secretary of the Treasury of Puerto Rico, Custodian of Alien Property, Comptroller of the Currency, etc., *were to discharge all debts.*

51. "Charges Against Board of Governors of the Federal Reserve Bank System, The Comptroller of the Currency and Secretary of the United States Treasury brought by Congressman Louis T. McFadden, May 23, 1933, Co-Chair of House Banking Committee, US Congressional Record, pp. 4055-4058"

52 The Naturalization Act of 1935. More deceitful efforts to entrap American Nationals and claim that they were "US citizens" subject to the whims of the "US CONGRESS".

53. 49 Statute 3097 Treaty Series 881 (Convention on Rights and Duties of States) December 26, 1933 — enacted as a result of the bankruptcies, both national and international, by the US CONGRESS — newly redefined to operate the UNITED STATES, INC. — **replaced all "statutory law"** (Federal Code and State Statutes) **with international law.** That is, the bankrupted United States of America, Inc. continued to function in reorganization under Federal Code, but the UNITED STATES,

INC., operated by the IMF, operates under the Uniform Commercial Code and International Admiralty jurisdiction.

54. Social Security Act, 1935. **Contrives** under conditions of conceit and non-disclosure **to register** everyone applying for any job, public or private, and to conscript them under these conditions to act as unpaid "voluntary" **Withholding Agents** in behalf of the Puerto Rican Estate Trusts set up "in their names".

55. U.S. Congressional Record Proceedings and Debates of the 76th Congress, Monday August 19, 1940, Third Session, Debate of Honorable Judge Thorkelson. — "Steps Toward British Union, A World State, and International Strife." — Part 1".

56. Alien Registration Act, 1940 – mandated registration of the names of all living Americans to create estate trusts operating under their names in foreign maritime and admiralty jurisdictions.

57. Buck Act, 1940 —"enfranchised" the ESTATES of American Nationals as "dual citizens" of The United States of America, and the corporate United States — and their respective franchises of the UNITED STATES, INC. operated as "STATES of States" (See UCC 1-308 Definitions) allowed this "enfranchisement" to stand as an excuse for claims of ownership and controlling interest in the assets of the individual ESTATE trusts — including the living men and women as slaves, and their private property as chattels still presumed to be "surety" for the debts of the United States of America, Inc. owed for the governmental services performed by the UNITED STATES, INC.

58. The Bretton Woods Accords, Inclusive, 1944, succeeded until 1971 in partial restoration of the Gold and Silver Standard, and as a secondary result, **ceded control** of all the agencies, assets, departments, logos, symbols, etc. to the UNITED NATIONS and its International Monetary Fund (IMF) agency doing business as the UNITED STATES. All STATE OF ALASKA offices are in fact UN corporate offices.

59. ***Hooven & Allison Vs. Evatt,*** 65 SCt.870, 880,321 U.S 652,89 L.Ed.12, 52 (1945) conclusively affirmed that there are t*wo (2) distinctly different United States* with TWO OPPOSITE FORMS OF GOVERNMENTS.

60. United Nations Charter, 1946. (Note, the commercial company d.b.a. UNITED NATIONS existed *prior* to the city-state being chartered as the "United Nations".)

61. Administrative Procedures Act (1946) provides statutory admission that *the ESTATES of American Nationals are the priority creditors of the United States of America, Inc.* and provides that *American Nationals* deemed to be civil executors and "federal contracting officers" administering their own ESTATES *are enabled to bring administrative claims against the United States of America, Inc. assets and also against the UNITED STATES.* This is where we got *two court systems* with differently styled names— **"The US District Court"** and **"THE US DISTRICT COURT"** for example. This was the remedy offered to the victims of the first fraud for the **second** fraud carried out against them by the UNITED NATIONS and the US Bankruptcy Trustee, when they rolled the assets of the individual *foreign situs* trusts into Roman Inferior ESTATE trusts. *Like the first remedy, this second remedy was never delivered to the people.* The perpetrator banking cartels which were by now funding both the Courts and the COURTS ordered their employees *to not recognize the standing* and identities *of the American Nationals,* conveniently laying claim to their ESTATES without providing remedy to them for the *theft of controlling interest* in their assets and misappropriation of their good faith and credit.

62. ***MILOSZEWSKI v. SEARS ROEBUCK,*** 346 F.Supp. 119 (1972)(2). [Outside of Constitutional authority is 100% private authority – NO lawful authority. 18 USC 2381-85 Treason - Sedition.] OPINION, FOX, Chief Judge (U.S. District

Court of Michigan): "A mere statement of this fact may not seem very significant; **corporations**, after all, **are not supposed to exercise the governmental powers with which the Bill of Rights is concerned.** But this has been radically changed by the emergence of **the public-private state.** Today private institutions do exercise governmental power; more, indeed, than 'government' itself .... **We have two governments in America, one under the Constitution and a much greater one** *not* **under the Constitution.** In short, the inapplicability of our Bill of Rights is one of the crucial facts of American life today." In fact, **American Nationals are owed the Bill of Rights** as they always have been. **"US citizens" are** *NOT* **owed the Bill of Rights.** The problem is that *we have all been self-interestedly mis-identified as "US citizens"; a crime known as "personage"* carried out against us by individuals and corporations in our employment and under contract to provide governmental services.

63. Foreign Sovereign Immunity Act, 1976. This releases all "State" laws and statutes specifically to the Uniform Commercial Code (maritime law). The corporate franchises calling themselves "States" continue to publish their own copyrighted version of the Uniform Commercial Code with addendums and label it as "Statutes" but these have no actual enabling clause.

64. Title 22 USC, Chapter 11, *all public officials designated foreign agents.*

65. 22 CFR 92, 12-92.31 "Foreign Relationship" requires an oath of office, and Title 8 USC 1481 states that once an oath of office is taken, *citizenship is relinquished.* As a result, when American Nationals are arbitrarily defined as "US citizens" and harassed by agents of the corporate United States and the UNITED STATES, INC. into acting as "Withholding Agents"; "Federal Contracting Agents"; or members of the Armed Forces, or as Federal Employees of any stamp, they temporarily and **for as long as they continue to act "in office"** lose the protections

and benefits of their birthright citizenship. This **"presumption of employment"** is often used by the corporate administrative tribunals to defraud and abuse American Nationals who are owed all the protections of The Constitution for the united States of America and the United Nations Declaration of Human Rights and also good faith service under contract.

66. Title 28 USC 3002, Section 15 (A), "United States" is a Federal Corporation, ***not a government,*** including the Judicial Procedural Section.

67. Court Registry Investment System Charter and Operations Manuel.

68. Committee on Uniform Securities Identification Procedures Minutes and Publications.

69. The Federal Prison Industry, Inc. Charter, d.b.a. UNICOR

70. The American Bar Association Style Manual.

71. Black's Law Dictionary, Fifth Edition.

72. Title 28 USC, Chapter 176, Federal Debt Collection Procedure — **places all courts** formerly operated by the United States of America, Inc. **in equity and commerce venues** under the International Monetary Fund, that is, **in receivership** and acting as corporate tribunals of the IMF, including "STATE" franchise courts.

73. UNITED STATES is a commercial corporation chartered in France by the International Monetary Fund, an agency of the UNITED NATIONS chartered by the Vatican.

74. Maxims of Law including "Fraud vitiates everything."

75. Universal Postal Treaty for the Americas 2010.

76. Burton's Legal Thesaurus, 5th Edition.

7

Where To Now?

Since issuing the FINAL JUDGMENT AND CIVIL ORDERS people have asked, now what? We are not standing in the Shoes of the Fishermen. All we can provide is an educated opinion offered in goodwill to the American people. Here is what we would do:

As individuals: know who you are and take action accordingly. Are you a birthright American National? Or are you rightly considered a "US citizen"? If you are a "US citizen" is it a permanent or temporary condition of employment?

Federal employees and members of the active duty military are considered "US citizens" during their employment, but they have the absolute right to quit their jobs or void their contracts (military service) if they are required to act in any manner contrary to the Law of the Land, known as "The Constitution for the united States of America", while on the land.

All American Negroes are similarly considered "US citizens" because the individual states did not act to formally recognize their State Citizenship at the end of the Civil War; however, this condition can be addressed in a number of ways. First, the corporate United States has guaranteed "equal civil rights" — equal to the rights of American Nationals, which includes the right to refuse any claims made by the corporate United States upon you, your persons, or your ESTATES. Second, you can push the reorganized and lawful state legislatures to formally recognize your equal status as Americans born on the land of the American states. That should have been done 150 years ago, but better late than never.

"Foreign" Welfare Recipients — Americans are considered to be "foreigners" with respect to the corporate United States and anyone receiving welfare benefits is considered to be a "US citizen", however, because these programs have been funded with American credit obtained under conditions of fraud and often have been entirely paid for by the recipients as a group (as in the case of Social Security), some other compelling basis would have to be established before the corporate United States could convincingly claim American welfare recipients as "US citizens".

Retirees – the corporate United States will no doubt attempt to claim that American Retirees owed Social Security Insurance coverage are "welfare recipients" receiving "benefits" (see above). Individual retirees need to object to this "interpretation" of their status and give notice to the Social Security Administration that it is their understanding that Social Security is and was a retirement insurance program that they paid into and are vested in, and not in any way welfare or benefit of any Public Charitable Trust. This is just more self-interested deceit. American workers paid for every drop of their retirement insurance coverage and are grandfathered in once vested, just as with any other **private** insurance program. **Receipt of Social Security payments does not provide any claim against your status as an American National.** If the Social Security Administration goes bankrupt, the corporate United States will be charged as secondary, and so on up the food chain.

Obamacare – is a brazen attempt to corner the market on medical insurance by the federal corporation. Ask yourselves — does Blue Cross have any right to "tax" me or force me to buy insurance coverage from them? If not, neither does E PLURIBUS UNUM THE UNITED STATES OF AMERICA, Inc. Just say, "No." I am not a "US citizen" and I am not obligated to pay or obey.

Internal Revenue / IRS — these are two separate agencies, the first representing the Federal Reserve System, the second representing the International Monetary Fund. They act in two separate roles. The first agency operates a debt account, using nine digits separated by dashes: 123-45-6789, and *is owed moderate service fees* for providing public services. The second agency *owes you a lot of money and is obligated to pay any and all debts that your ESTATE may owe* drawn from a credit account using nine digits without dashes: 123456789. These two agencies work together to defraud you, *but you have the right to act as the Civil Executor on the Land of your own ESTATE, and once you have proven who you are, you have every right to tell the holder of the debt (Internal Revenue Service) to bill the holder of the credit (IRS) and discharge any taxes, tithes, or fees owed by the ESTATE.*

State Legislators – enter your **public offices** immediately, take valid oaths to the "Alaska state" and the "living Alaskan people" — or whatever other state, such as "illinois" and people "Illionoians" you believe you represent — and act together as an **unincorporated** Body Politic to demand

(1) the release of all land within the state's geographically defined borders that are not specifically granted for "federal" use under permit (such as "federal courthouses", military bases, arsenals, etc. that are traditionally allocated to the use of the "federal government"),

(2) recognize that the "United States senators" are still under their original obligation to the state legislatures — they work for you and are accountable to the state, not the federal corporation, not the corporate United States, and not the IMF. Demand that they account for their actions and inactions and remove them from public office if they have failed to abide by "The Constitution for the united States of America" and "The Alaska Statehood Compact" (just substitute the name of your state),

(3) recognize that "US congress members" are similarly directly accountable to the people of the state and demand that

they immediately act to release all false claims against state and private property assets that have been made via the use of legal fiction entities however constructed, together with all false titles to land and other assets held under color of law,

(4) recognize only "state banks" operated under state control and force all "national banks" to submit to state banking rules in order to do business in your state — and make sure those rules are explicit in denying the use of "off book" accounts and other practices not allowed by Basel I, II, and III,

(5) force all "courts" currently operating in your state to declare exactly who or what is operating them, and in what jurisdiction they are operating, and for what purpose(s) they are operating and make them openly, freely, and officially declare their nature and status so that people are no longer hoodwinked,

(6) void the charters of all municipalities and boroughs operating in your state that have been issued under the auspices of the United States of America (minor) or the UNITED STATES; these entities are under foreign obligation and have been established under conditions of fraud based on semantic deceit; so provide substitute issuance/ of city and other government unit charters as appropriate.

Note that inhabiting an American public office requires you to act with 100% commercial liability and according to The Constitution for the united States of America. As a result, you wield ultimate power, but to exercise this power you must also accept ultimate responsibility. Also recognize that your acceptance of public office does not confer any special magic power or serve to make you "more equal" than any other birthright American. All Americans who accept the responsibility of a civil office may exercise it, because the **entire** power of the civil government is vested in **every** American without exception.

You cannot claim any control over public assets based

on your public office while operating in a private capacity.
For example, you cannot sign a valid contract selling the Alaska
state's oil resources while enjoying any limited liability whatsoever,
and you cannot make any such agreements in conflict of interest.

Governors of states — See above.

"US" congress members and "senators" — Find a
distinct and unequivocal name for the corporate United States
and end the semantic deceits and crimes that have been
perpetuated as a result of this purposeful confusion at law. When
you are operating the Municipal government, or the Insular States
government, either one, make it clear to everyone everywhere
that that is the capacity in which you are acting and do not allow
any sloppy interpretation of your authorities and actions to bleed
over and impact American Nationals.

Judges, Lawyers, Court Clerks, Judicial Councils —
Once you've read the rest of this document, it should be apparent
that you are not required to be a member of the Bar Association.
We suggest tearing up your Bar and/or BAR cards and forming a
state-based professional association that accomplishes the
worthy and positive functions of such an organization without the
corruption and negative elements. Nobody is prevented from
practicing law in America and never has been, nor is anyone
prevented from offering **lawful** service. **Set up your own courts
as loyal Americans, include service under American
Common Law, and go to it.** The Bar Associations have long
functioned as "closed union shops" and in violation of Taft-Hartley.
Bust them for it.

The original **13th Amendment** to The Constitution for the
united States of America does NOT prevent you from serving
your country or from plying your trade. It simply prevents you
from serving a foreign government (that of the city state of
Westminster) and accepting titles from that government as a Bar
Association Member. So, purge your ranks of liars and traitors,

do the right thing as Americans, and you'll be fine. Otherwise, pack your belongings and go. You have three years as of July 1, 2013 to settle your affairs and leave, provided that you do no harm to anyone else and do not infringe upon the material interests of any American National in the meantime and do not operate as an Undeclared Foreign Agent on our soil. If you cause any such trouble, you will be immediately arrested and deported at once.

Bankers - Obviously, if you've been operating a "national" bank without the American nation on American soil and proposing to conscript Americans as debt slaves via the self-interested presumption that American Nationals are "US citizens", you are in a heap of trouble, and need to quickly, quietly, and determinedly make changes to recognize the interests of the American Nationals in their own private accounts, and to admit all off-book and escrow and demand accounts the bank has held or processed for federal corporations "in the name of" American Nationals.

All fiat money systems based on "Notes" whether "Federal Reserve Notes" or "US Treasury Notes" are illegal in America, aka, The United States of America composed of 50 organic states, and you are under complete demand to provide legal tender based on gold and silver coin standards. Otherwise, your clientele will be strictly limited to "US citizens" and you will be under full obligation to completely reveal . . .

(1) the difference between "US citizens" and "American Nationals" and precluded from offering service to any American National;

(2) required to reprove the citizenship status of all clients and that they have adopted that status knowingly, willingly, and under conditions of complete, explicit, and fully discussed disclosure of the consequences as well as any benefits,

(3) honor the living status of American Nationals and never again create accounts merely "in the name" of any living man or

woman born on the land of the American states based on "representations" made in their behalf,

(4) commit no act of false advertising, such as advertising "loans" based on the customer's own credit. All national banks operating facilities on the land of the states will be obliged to conform to state standards and function according to "The Constitution for the united States of America" when addressing or offering services of any kind to American Nationals.

The circumstance that American Nationals have suffered in having no money with which to pay debts is entirely the fault of the private, for-profit corporations under contract to provide these governmental services and the Department of Defense Financial Services Administration. Any bank proposing to offer service to the American Nationals must provide interest free commodity based real money subject to the gold and silver coin standard, not corporate I.O.U.'s, not fiat "debt notes", and cannot charge any interest, make any loan, or offer to indebt any American National or state on the basis of failure to provide such service.

Military Officers, Police, Provost Marshals, Civilian Employees of DOD - Remember who you actually work for and make no mistake. There are two different populations being served. American Nationals pay for your services and are owed your good faith service and dedication. "US citizens" are allowed to be present on the land of the organic states, but operate (at present) under a different government and are not owed the same protections, rights, and guarantees. All American Nationals are owed all protections of their national trust indenture and commercial service contract known as "The Constitution for the united States of America" and any law, rule, statute, or code serving to infringe upon them or their material rights in contravention of **their** Constitution is a violation of the Law of the Land and the Supreme Law of the Land which you are obligated to observe, honor, and protect under contract.

The following is a transcript of an original handwritten document delivered to Judge Thomas F. Hogan, and as copies to other parties. The transcript is provided to expedite reading comprehension and ease of communication only.

8

Writ of Assistance and Affidavit of Truth

RA 393 427 517 US — June 3, 2014

To: US DISTRICT COURT / US District Court
CLERK OF COURT / Clerk of Court
US TRUSTEES / US Trustees
OFFICERS OF THE COURT / Officers of the Court
JUDGE THOMAS F. HOGAN / Judge Thomas F. Hogan

From: anna-maria, private attorney, all rights explicitly reserved.

RE: Asset Claims, IRS, Mortgage Claims, Bankruptcy Claims, etc.

Dear Sir(s):

As you can see from the fact that this is a handwritten Writ of Assistance, I am not a juristic person, my estate is not naturally a juristic estate, nor am I the subject of a juristic estate. I am not a DEFENDANT of any kind. As a mortal woman, I am unable to franchise myself, even if I wanted to.

Yesterday, I received a call from Ms. Tonya Rhames who introduced herself (IRS) and attempted to intimidate me with threats related to what she inferred is an ongoing Federal Grand Jury inquiry into "me" and "my affairs". She seemed to think I should be willing to meet with her even though she was unwilling to put her questions into writing and according to agency policy — so she said — was unable to provide me with records she had questions about, even though the whole conversation and fact that she was talking to me implied that the records were mine and that preserving my privacy from myself COULD NOT logically be an issue.

Last June 4, 2013, I entered special appearance before the US TAX COURT in Anchorage, Alaska. I appeared in the flesh, clearly stated my whole given name, and the proper way to address me. I informed the court that I was not a "withholding agent" or other employee, ship's warrant officer, etc., and provided material evidence in support. If the judge considered me the DEFENDANT he certainly did not address me as such during the hearing, and I never heard another word from the US TAX COURT. I never received any correspondence addressed to me, either, as I told Ms. Rhames.

It is not my intention to insult the US DISTRICT COURT or the IRS or anyone else concerned, but I must observe that it is not possible in equity to claim criminal or civil contempt of court based on non-performance of court orders not addressed to you and issued in foreign jurisdictions.

I might have also observed to Ms. Rhames that as I know for sure that I am not a Withholding Agent, Ship's Warrant Officer, or other employee of the UNITED STATES corporation, it is extremely inappropriate for any IRS personnel to suggest that I sign paperwork under condition of penalty of perjury claiming that I am, or that I am under any obligation to engage in such criminal acts.

When I was still a baby in my cradle unscrupulous men merely claiming to "represent" me enfranchised my given name without my knowledge or consent. They used this device to lay claim to my earthly estate under color of law, claimed that I was "missing—presumed lost at sea", claimed that their corporation was my beneficiary, misappropriated my credit, and moved the "ANNA

MARIA RIEZINGER ESTATE" to Puerto Rico — placing it under the control of a foreign government, that of the United States of America (minor) — a "union" of "American" "states" more normally thought of as "federal territories and possessions".

This is known as a "reverse trust scheme" in which a person posing as a trustee contrives to cheat the beneficiary and lay claim to the trust assets to benefit themselves directly or a third party they are colluding with, to share the spoils. It is just as criminal now when practiced by giant corporations as it was in the nineteenth century when it was popular among British butlers.

The privately owned and operated "Federal Reserve" banking cartel operating an agency calling itself the WISCONSIN STATE BOARD OF HEALTH approached my Mother under the pretense of recording my birth and registered it instead. The affect of this "voluntary contract" was never fully disclosed nor discussed; the very existence of any contract impacting my estate, my nationality, or my controlling interests, was concealed from my Mother and her ignorance guaranteed mine as well. I couldn't object to a contract, if I didn't know it existed, could I?

Thus a privately owned agency of a privately owned corporation — both deceptively named to mislead people into thinking they were part of the legitimate government — secured an undisclosed claim against me and my earthly estate. The Federal Reserve banks then used my collateral as the basis to issue "bonds" — Birth Certificate Bonds, and claimed that my earthly estate was chattel standing as "surety" backing the debts of the Federal Reserve and the United States of America, **Incorporated**, a bankrupt governmental services corporations undergoing Chapter 11 reorganization.

All this was done without disclosure, without notice, and without consent.

Thus the first step of the Reverse Trust Fraud was exercised against me and my estate by international bankers. Their excuse for this unspeakable fraud and deceit was that still other unscrupulous men, politicians claiming to represent "me", gave them permission.

On March 6, 1933, politicians acting as officers of private, for profit corporations named after the organic States of the Union created by the Articles of Confederation and operating as the "State of_____" franchises of the bankrupt United States of America, **Incorporated**, readily agreed to let the Federal Reserve use "the good faith and credit" of "their states and the citizenry thereof" as collateral backing the debts of their governmental services corporation in Chapter 11.

The fact that their "States" were all private corporations merely named after the organic states of the union and their "citizens" were merely *foreign situs* trusts named after living Americans, didn't prevent the Federal Reserve from "misunderstanding on purpose" and advancing improper claims against the real assets of the organic states and the American People.

The swindlers had stolen our identity, commandeered our rightful government by stealthy usurpation, and gained control of our credit cards by a process of semantic deceits based on similar names and undisclosed commercial claims. The swindlers at the "State" level were happy enough to help the "federal" level crooks in exchange for "federal revenue sharing".

In 1944, the International Monetary Fund booted up the UNITED STATES, yet another governmental services corporation, and took over the juicy contracts and assets of the United States of America, Incorporated — right down to the US Department of Commerce and the corporate flag. The IMF, an agency of the UN, has been running things ever since.

As a second step in the Great Fraud, the bankruptcy Trustee named by the creditors of the United States of America,

Incorporated, — the Secrectary of the Treasury of Puerto Rico — created Roman Inferior Trusts <u>also named after</u> living Americans and moved all the ESTATES to Puerto Rico, where they have been plundered at will.

Legal conventions since Roman times mandate that living people <u>must be described</u> or denoted in <u>all small letter names</u>. Under Roman Civil Law they only lose that status when they become <u>debtors,</u> at which point a free man partially loses his status and is named using upper and lower case style conventions. <u>Slaves are named using all capital letters</u>.

Some people try to pretend that these naming conventions are "a matter of semantics" but all these Roman Inferior Trusts named after Americans and "presumed" to contain all our earthly assets are administered under <u>Roman Civil Law</u> — so the naming conventions mean what they meant two thousand years ago, and that's why they are used at all. That is also the reason that the Roman Curia is responsible for these ESTATES and the reason that the Vatican Chancery Court is the supreme court of record and equity claims brought against these ESTATES — not the "US Supreme Court" and certainly not the "US DISTRICT COURT".

I have brought my claim of life before the Vatican Chancery Court and redeemed my ESTATE; having overcome all claims of beneficial interest and all claims of controlling interest, I have presented myself as the unique beneficiary of all ESTATE assets, which are owed to me as Caesar upon the land of the organic states.

This is because my forefathers vested the entire <u>civil government</u> in each and every inhabitant of the organic states. Each American has more civil authority on the land than the entire "federal government" and when the federal government acts as a corporation in commerce it has only the rights and protections of any other commercial corporation.

Neither the UNITED STATES corporation nor its employees nor its agents enjoy any immunity from prosecution for criminal acts — including fraud, extortion, unlawful conversion, and inland piracy.

As the unique beneficiary of the ESTATES named after me, I have told the Internal Revenue Service (which has the credit side of my account) to pay the IRS credit to balance out any alleged debts. This is essentially a matter of forcing the Federal Reserve to drop its claim that it is the beneficiary of my ESTATE(S), pay the IMF for governmental services it provided, and pay off all the debts and encumbrances the Federal Reserve charged against my credit and my ESTATE(S) via fraud.

It is clearly not my will to harm or defraud anyone. I come to equity as a creditor with clean hands and as a beneficiary of a sacred trust who has innocently suffered great harm at the hands of persons owing me nothing but good faith, service, and protection.

I require the return of my property — my controlling interest, my name, my credit, my bank accounts, my organic state, free of debt or encumbrances accrued by the false beneficiaries or others claiming to "represent" me or my interests, including any public trustees operating in breach of trust.

Let's make this clear — every single member of the American Bar Association and the British Bar Association and the entire City State of Westminster owes **me** "perpetual peace and amity" as an "ally" owed the "protection" of the British Crown "in perpetuity". That obligation is not erased by the convenient deceit of pretending that I am someone else or in this case, some "thing" else.

Any assault against me, my vessels in commerce, or my ESTATE whatsoever is a violation of international treaty and a war crime against a non-combatant civilian.

170

The "US DISTRICT COURT" needs to get the message. If you want to get paid, you need to expedite the "re-venue" of American assets back to Americans. The "US Attorney" needs to get the message, too. There is no future in oppressing and defrauding your _employers_. There is only a very real jail or deportation order waiting for those who are slow to accept correction. The same is true for the IRS, which stands to suffer large fines if it continues to bring false claims in equity.

Nobody is helped by any continued "misunderstanding" or hostility except those responsible for creating, promoting, and prolonging all this _fraud_. If you want to be identified as criminals, then sail on. Otherwise, it is well past time to reverse course, render aid and assistance, and make correction.

Now, I realize that I come across as an angry litigant — but instead of that, I am an outraged seeker of _peace_, merely determined to end the current fraud and predation and make transition as painless as possible.

I require the assistance of the US Courts and all their officers to return my property including all elements protected by the national trust indenture included in the Preamble and Bill of Rights of the original equity agreement known as "The Constitution for the united States of America".

I also require the US Courts and their officers to take NOTICE of the situation discussed herein, to assess, evaluate, and combat the corruption and predatory practices that have been used to defraud, rob, and falsely indebt the American People — me, among them. Be aware that while the UNITED STATES is owed money for services it has provided, the debtor responsible for paying the bill is the Federal Reserve, not individual Americans who have been defrauded.

All tax bills must be properly addressed to the Internal Revenue Service (Federal Reserve) requesting payment on the account in behalf of the IRS. The IMF should be direct billing and so should the IRS when it engages as a bill collector. There should be clear and open understanding among all parties including the officers of the "US DISTRICT COURT" of who the real parties of interest are and who owes who, how much, and why.

At this time, the Federal Reserve, the Department of Defense, and the North American Water and Power Alliance owe the American People in excess of 20 trillion "dollars" worth of purloined assets and misappropriated private credit, and that is just the tip of the iceberg.

It is necessary, urgent, and right that all improper administration ceases and all collection of presumed debts from individual living Americans ceases. The Federal Reserve constructed this entire fraud scheme. It is time for the Federal Reserve to pay its debts, directly. The Internal Revenue Service is knowingly or in ignorance continuing to bring claims against individual ESTATES under the false presumption that they are sureties for the debts piled up by these fraudsters.

The "US DISTRICT COURT" acting as a "federal" — that is, IMF, debt collection agency operating under "federal debt collection procedures" and freely allowing itself to "write the unwritten law" of Law Merchant as it goes is a big part of the problem.

In 1845 via the Treaty of the Verona, the then-Pope and the British King representing the interests of the British Crown agreed to undermine the American government. The King issued Letters of Marque and Reprisal to the members of the Bar Association commissioning them to act as privateers and offering them protection. Those letters operated in perpetuity — until 2013, when they were extinguished and the Treaty of Verona repudiated.

The "US DISTRICT COURT" and its officers have been given copies of the July 11, 2013 "Motu Proprio" issued by Pope

172

Francis acting as the Global Estate Trustee and signed "FRANCISCUS". Anyone and everyone involved in the court system worldwide is now 100% liable for their acts and omissions. That includes the "US SUPREME COURT JUSTICES" down to the lowliest clerks. The order took full effect on September 1, 2013.

Thus it is no longer a matter of whether the Bar Associations want to be nice guys or not. If they continue to expedite the fraud against the American People and to use their office to confiscate private property under these conditions, the Bar Associations will be outlawed and their members prosecuted, fined, and/or jailed as criminals — worldwide.

This news (and the changes in operations) has been slow in distribution, no doubt because some people don't want the feeding frenzy to end, and others, like US Attorney Karen Loeffler, are afraid of all the things they have already done and what reparations will require.

By addressing this Writ of Assistance and Affidavit of Truth to JUDGE THOMAS F. HOGAN, the Director of the Administrative Office of the US Courts, and publishing this Writ and Affidavit under edict of Notice — "Notice to Principals is Notice to Agents. Notice to Agents is Notice to Principals." — it is my intention to secure prompt aid and assistance from this office and all officers subject to his guidance and administration, or failing that, to exercise my standing to bring complaint and claim.

The Treaty of Westminster (1784) has been properly invoked by one having the right and standing to invoke it. The fraud, which has no statute of limitations, has been described. The entire "maritime government" including the office of JUDGE THOMAS F. HOGAN has been informed and provided with a copy of the referenced "Motu Proprio" and the Final Judgment and Civil Orders issued in April, 2014.

There can be no misunderstanding and no continuance of the legal presumptions which have been used to defraud Americans for three generations, and to impose debt slavery upon them.

Specific Assistance Required

1. Administrative direction given to all US Courts regarding the fraud which has been practiced against the American People, directing all such courts and tribunals to set free all those jailed under the false presumption of "US citizenship"—that is, all Americans who are not naturally subject to maritime jurisdiction or actual employees of the UNITED STATES Corporation and who have otherwise not freely chosen to undergo the process to become "Federal Citizens" stipulated in US Statute at Large 2, Revised Statute 2165.

2. Administrative direction given to all US Courts regarding the true parties of interest in all cases brought by either the Internal Revenue Service in behalf of the Federal Reserve or the IRS in behalf of the International Monetary Fund, and holding harmless all individual ESTATES and unincorporated sole proprietors, and partnerships and associations operating on the land or in behalf of the land's inhabitants.

3. Administrative direction given to all US Courts regarding the limitations of their jurisdictions, and the responsibilities of both Plaintiffs and Attorneys when presenting claims under Law Merchant and Admiralty — specifically, there must be a clearly identified injured party who is NOT the attorney in the case taking full responsibility under commercial liability for making the charge or issuing the complaint, and in Admiralty cases there must be a valid maritime contract in evidence which is freely and fully disclosed and discussed by all parties concerned. Such contracts cannot be presumed to exist or to be valid absent a finding of true maritime subject matter and voluntary, fully disclosed, in-kind, equitable, two-party contract having been executed by people or persons competent to enter into contract — that is, no "third party" contracts

made by "representatives" or "trustees" or "donors" on behalf of any individual or more to the point, any individual ESTATE presumed to exist, without open scrutiny by the court to ascertain the authority, identity, and capacity of such representatives and the appropriateness of the contracts they have entered into "on the behalf" of other parties. It must be clearly understood by all US Courts that <u>contracts executed in breach of trust are universally invalid and cannot be enforced.</u>

4. Administrative direction given to the US Attorney's Office in Anchorage, Alaska, and to the US DISTRICT COURT in Anchorage, Alaska, and to US ATTORNEY KAREN LOEFFLER of Anchorage, Alaska, instructing these persons to stand down, cease and desist, all inappropriate assaults upon the individual American Nationals and their rightfully reclaimed and redeemed ESTATE(S), which are all allies of the Crown owed perpetual peace from Westminster and all protections they are guaranteed by treaty and trust indenture. It must be understood and clearly communicated to the US Courts that the ESTATES of the living Americans and their private business enterprises and social organizations as well as all property rightfully belonging to their organic geographically defined states, including the Alaska state, are in <u>safe keeping</u> only, <u>not subject</u> to the Crown, and owed all aid and assistance from officers of the Crown. All living individuals and their ESTATES must be set free and all interest in their property must be released from any presumption that they are or ever were "surety" for the debts of the United States of America, Incorporated, or ever legitimately "residents" of Puerto Rico, or "citizens of the UNITED STATES" ,etc., etc., etc., [— — claims made under conditions of fraud —] and with the understanding that these individuals and their ESTATES are NOT subject to the Crown, NOT subject to the jurisdiction of the United States of America (minor) and not subject to representations made "in their behalf" or contracts made "in their behalf" by any incorporated entity whatsoever that has merely claimed to

"represent" them on the basis of undisclosed contracts obtained under conditions of fraud, semantic deceit and coercion including armed force and monopoly inducement.

5. Administrative direction given to the US Courts advising and instructing them that the "Federal Reserve Corporation" has operated as a criminal syndicate and that the International Monetary Fund, Inc. has colluded with them to plunder the "public trusts" created by the Federal Reserve's "complex regulatory scheme" and that both these entities are subject to liquidation and disposal of their assets in payment of reparations owed to the American states, the American People, and others around the globe who have been terrorized and pillaged by those operating these legal fictions. The officers of the US Courts must be instructed to come to the assistance of the victims and to deny bankruptcy protection to both the Federal Reserve and the International Monetary Fund and also to the Trust Management Organizations and agencies and corporations these entities operate, to the extent that they have knowingly and willingly participated in the fraud.

6. Administrative direction given to the office of JUDGE TIMOTHY M. BURGESS and US ATTORNEY KAREN LOEFFLER, directing them to immediately order the release of the living man james-leroy:jensen, jr. and the living woman robin-louise:jensen from false arrest related to a fraudulent tax claim arising from purposeful misadministration of their ESTATE(S) which the US DISTRICT COURT accepted and prosecuted as account # 3:09-cr-00108 TMB 1 and 2, and also order payment of reparations owed these individuals and their ESTATE(S). The jensens rightfully informed the COURT of their standing and identity as American Nationals and objected to being misidentified by the COURT as "withholding agents" or other officials or employees of the UNITED STATES. They subsequently acted under condition of gross coercion to discharge the purported tax debts, thereby proving beyond reasonable doubt that any tax debt owed by their ESTATE(S) was fictitious in nature and the result of the

failure of the Internal Revenue Service (Federal Reserve) employees to do the bookkeeping and transfer credit to pay the IRS (International Monetary Fund). Like millions of other Americans the jensens were prevented from accessing the credit side of their ESTATE trust because the Federal Reserve claimed to be the Beneficiary of their ESTATE(S). They were misidentified and mischaracterized as public employees in the same way that their private estates were unlawfully converted into public trusts by fraud upon the probate courts. The jensens are the victims of crime, not the perpetrators responsible for it. They have been held in private "federal" "correctional facilities" for over a year under conditions of known false arrest. The US DISTRICT COURT and its officers are complicit in the fraud at this point and responsible for providing full remedy at equity and full cure and maintenance under admiralty law to the jensens. They have been given all Due Process including Final Notice and Notice of Dishonor in both jurisdictions, and the US DISTRICT COURT and its OFFICERS will be found both culpable and liable for this circumstance if PROMPT administrative action is not taken to correct this situation in full. As there is not known monetary standard for the value of an individual's life and time on earth, settlement is stipulated in the amount of $100,000.00 USD per individual, per day that the false arrest and incarceration continues in this case. Without putting too sharp a point on it, if it is the job and aim of the "US DISTRICT COURT" to collect funds owed to the "UNITED STATES", it should confine its efforts to Internal Revenue Service employees — real ones — and bring a swift end to the incarceration of innocent Third Parties.

7. Administrative direction to the US Courts recognizing the fact that the Roman Curia holds authority over all aspects of Roman Civil Law including its interpretation, that Roman Inferior Trusts also known as "Cestui Que Vie" Trusts, are uniquely formed as creations of the Roman Civil Law and to the extent that their administration is necessary, it remains under the Roman Civil Law

and under the authority of the Roman Curia to define, interpret, and ultimately to dictate the administration of these trusts in whatever venue they appear. Accordingly, all the living Americans and their organic states which were "redefined" by the Secretary of rhe Treasury of Puerto Rico and removed there "for safe-keeping" are all Roman Inferior Trusts, they all exist and operate under the rules established by the Roman Curia and are subject to the Vatican Chancery Court as the ultimate and final court of record and equity. The Vatican Chancery Court has explicitly determined and placed in the international record of all nations and venues of the international law its un-appeal-able decision awarding the beneficial and controlling interest in the individual ESTATE(S) to the Americans they are named after, and has also determined that the living Americans are "tax exempt" and that their "vessels in commerce" are "tax pre-paid". As a practical matter this means that "anna-maria of the house riezinger" is tax exempt from any claim of any "government" upon the land or sea, that the foreign situs trust dba "Anna Maria Riezinger" is tax pre-paid, and the Roman Inferior Trust "ANNA MARIA RIEZINGER" is similarly tax pre-paid as a result of pre-existing contracts owed by the international banking cartels and governmental services corporations they operate under contract. It is, and since 1933, has been, literally impossible for any of these entities to owe ANY "tax debts" whatsoever. Every single case that the US TAX COURT and the US DISTRICT COURT has processed since 1933 against these individuals and their estate trusts related to "tax debts" has been tainted by fraud and are null and void, ab initio.

8. Administrative direction to the US Courts advising them of these facts above and instructing them to release all living Americans being held for any tax related offenses whatsoever, and ordering the immediate discharge of any claims offered by the Internal Revenue Service or the IRS against all and any "vessels in commerce" — trusts, transmitting utilities, foundations, etc., —

operated by American Nationals or their organic states. As astounding as this may seem, it is merely part of what is owed. The IMF dba "IRS" should be advised to directly bill the Internal Revenue Service (FEDERAL RESERVE) and the Internal Revenue Service should be advised that the buck for tax debts stops at the Federal Reserve. Bringing claims against individual living Americans or their trusts, transmitting utilities, or other commercial "vessels" for alleged "tax debts" is a criminal act subject to prosecution.

9. Similarly, I require your assistance and the assistance of your office(s) to provide administrative direction to the US Courts instructing them to vigorously prosecute public utility companies which deny electrical, telephone, or other such services to living Americans and their unincorporated sole proprietorships, partnerships, and associations for "non-payment" of utility bills under the pretense that these ESTATE trusts are "corporate parties" responsible for payment. In a corollary scam to that practiced by the Federal Reserve, the North American Water and Power Alliance has used the convenient excuse – "corporate entities are liable to pay for public utilities" — to bill the ESTATE(S) of living Americans — ignoring the fact that all the utility bills owed by these ESTATE(S) have been pre-paid since 1933. The utility companies have followed the practices of the IRS and Internal Revenue Service in purposefully misidentifying and mischaracterizing their "customers" and in the case of cooperatives, their "members" and continued to charge for utility services under the pretense that they are all corporate entities and that the True Trust beneficiaries are "unknown".

10. Similarly, I require assistance providing administrative directions to the US Courts including "State" franchise courts requiring reform of their presumptions and procedures and disposition of claims made by banks which have similarly and without full disclosure or consent unlawfully converted the private bank accounts including savings accounts and escrow accounts

owed to individual American Nationals on the pretense that these funds belong to the Puerto Rican ESTATE Trusts established "in the name" of individual living Americans inhabiting the organic state—geographically defined. This is merely another tentacle of the fraud and false claims and self-interested misrepresentation akin to all the rest that needs to be addressed.

11. Finally, I require assistance in the form of administrative direction to the US Courts providing them and their officers with the necessary information, instruction, and support to carry out these necessary reforms as stipulated in the enclosed Final Judgment and Civil Orders issued in April 2014. Over 10,000 copies of this handwritten (W)rit of Assistance and other documents accompanying would be insufficient without your understanding and cooperation in support of justice, law, and your own profession. Extreme perfidy and felony crimes are being committed every day under the auspices of the "US DISTRICT COURTS" and your Office which is responsible for their administration is uniquely culpable for this circumstance. In the presumption of innocence, it can be presumed that you, like millions of others, have been victimized, have paid "taxes" you didn't owe, utility bills, mortgages, and various other "debts" which were in fact pre-paid long ago. All your acts and the actions of your brethren operating the "State" and "US" courts can be presumed to be — however ignorant and mistaken — to have been in good faith, up until now, when decisions must be made and actions taken. As an individual you can yield to the facts and the logic self-evident in the history and public records, and you can take heed and listen to the Vatican Chancery Court — which has no reason to lie — or not, but be advised that this Writ of Assistance and Affidavit of Truth, handwritten by an American Great-Grandma who has no criminal history at all, has been published worldwide, and it will either stand for you or against you, depending on what you do now and the efforts that you make to ensure correction.

I affirm that in issuing this Writ of Assistance I am an ally in dire need upon the Holy Se(a) and that I have sacred commissions to fulfill in temporal capacities which will not wait; I similarly affirm that I have spoken the Truth, the whole Truth, and nothing but the Truth as I know it in this written form today, and that I have acted in good faith, friendship, without malice, evil intent, or any secretive purpose at all — and to this I also affirm that I am a known woman, recognized as the wife of a known man, a life-long peaceful inhabitant of the Alaska state or one of the other Several states as geographically defined and joined as The United States of America (major). I and my estates are natural and non-juristic, organic, retired, and beyond desire; the juristic ESTATE(S) that I am heir to and which I have redeemed, I affirm that they are identical in all material aspects (except name and number) to millions upon millions of other such ESTATE(S) and that none of the conditions, circumstances, or processes described are at all unique to me and mine: approximately 400 million inhabitants of the now-50 organic states have all been similarly mistreated and defrauded by privately owned and operated international banking cartels and the deceptively named governmental services corporations they have operated. The proof of everything I have said here is readily available on the public records cited in the Final Judgment and Civil Orders, to which I add 31 CFR 353-363 and 31 USC 1321 and 1322 and the Old Age Pension Act of 1939.

Most sincerely,

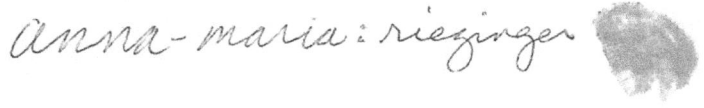

anna-maria:riezinger, non-negotiable autograph, all rights explicitly reserved

[autographed, thumbprinted, and sealed]

9

General Civil Orders - 1

June 10, 2014
Issued to All Members of the Domestic Police Forces, US Marshals Service, the Provost Marshal, Members of the American Bar Association and the American Armed Services

At the federal level, the American government has always been a *separate foreign international maritime jurisdiction* operating under contract to provide just two services: (1) **to protect** the assets of the national trust, and (2) **to perform** governmental services **for** the Several States — which in terms of international law are **all** recognized as sovereign nations.

The *equity contract* known as **The Constitution for the united States of America** makes it clear that the Several States contracted to form *a single governmental services agency* known as **The United States**. The contract designates in the Preamble and Bill of Rights *the assets to be held in trust* by the federal government comprising the trust indenture portion of the contract and also designates *the nineteen enumerated services* to be performed — and exactly what *"powers"* the States agreed to delegate to **The United States** and how they would pay for these services.

What isn't so widely known or appreciated is that *the governmental services company known as* **The United States** *was a privately owned and operated commercial company set up by Benjamin Franklin in 1754*. George Washington was actually the *11th "President"* of this Company, and the

1st President to take office after the receipt of the **"Constitution"** contract.

According to the 1824 Webster's Dictionary, at the time the original Constitution was written, the word **"federal"** was a synonym for **"contract"**. **All "constitutions" are affirmations of debt** — in this case, the debt that the States assumed when they created the federal government and *jointly agreed* to pay for the services that it would provide. The office of *"President"* is, and always has been, a uniquely *commercial office,* not a "Head of State".

Because the *federal governmental services company* is privately operated and owned, only *shareholders* known as *"electors"* have a real say in its elections and administration; only *"trustees"* known as *"members of Congress"* have the right to determine *how* the national trust assets are protected, though they are obligated as trustees to do a reasonable job of it, and *only the States have the right to complain* if the designated services aren't up to par.

The American people at large, known simply as *"inhabitants of the domestic states"* or *"State Citizens"* have always been a separate and distinct population apart from *"US citizens"* or *"Federal Citizens"* — and to these two groups *a third kind of "citizen"* was added in 1871, that of *"US citizen"*.

Following the Civil War, the *governmental services company* providing the services agreed to by the States, *reorganized as a corporation* d.b.a. the **"United States of America, Incorporated"** and published its Articles of Incorporation as the *"Constitution of the United States of America"*.

Unlike *"The Constitution for the united States of America",* the *"Constitution of the United States of America"* is a document peculiar to the new **"Municipal"** or

"City State" government **formed to administer the affairs of the District of Columbia and its federal territories and possessions.**

This *corporate "constitution"* provided for the creation of a new kind of **"Federal Citizen"** — a **"US Citizen"** — and from that point onward, from the perspective of *the new federal municipal government formed by the Act of 1871* — **American State Citizens** (the inhabitants of the domestic fifty states) were regarded as **"non-resident aliens"**. This same corporation, d.b.a. the "United States of America, Incorporated" (chartered in Delaware), began operating *two separate "governments"* at once — the *"municipal government of the District of Columbia"* and the *"federal government"* owed *to the States of the Union* — both under the auspices of the **"United States Congress"**.

These *semantic deceits* have given rise to endless confusions, usurpations, and criminality. These *General Civil Orders* address *some* of those issues which are most important at this time.

The Congress *ceased operating* as it was required by contract to operate, in **1860**. After December **1865**, it never again operated as an *unincorporated Body Politic* representing the States of the Union. The *"federal government"* has functioned ever since exclusively as an *incorporated commercial entity*, with an elected Board of Directors calling itself the **"US Congress"**. As such, the *"federal government"* is a for-profit commercial corporation like any other for-profit commercial corporation. It has no special status, *no immunity from prosecution*, and hasn't functioned as a governing body of a sovereign nation for 150 years.

To overcome this obvious difficulty the **"US Congress"** formed a *second "union of American states"* from the *"federal territories and possessions"*. From the Seven Insular States, including the "State of New Columbia" (District of Columbia), Guam, Puerto Rico, American Samoa, et alia, a *new nation* was formed, calling itself **"the United States of America"**, claiming separate national sovereignty.

Thus we have *the United States of America* comprised of the fifty organic States created by Statehood Compacts, and *the district United States;* both being administered under the direction of *the corporate Board of Directors* known as the **"US Congress"** — which has continued to act *solely* as the sovereign government of *the corporate United States*.

These *blatant semantic deceits* by officers of the federal corporation and officials of *the corporate United States* amount to *purposeful constructive fraud* against their *employers,* the American organic states. To try to overcome this obstacle, members of the **"US Congress"** contrived a *"complex regulatory scheme"* by which they established their *own* **"State" governments** and have tried to claim that they have been *"at war" with the American people,* while relying upon the organic states for their own sustenance, and have falsely claimed that they have established *"exclusive legislative jurisdiction"* over the original states of the Union by these acts of *self-interested fraud* carried out against their *employers* and benefactors.

Fraud has no statute of limitations.

The *governmental services corporations* have always been under commercial contract to provide services to the American people and have acted against their *employers,* **as employees**.

It is essential that *members of the Bar Associations; members of the "State" governments* which have been surreptitiously "redefined" to their detriment; *members of the domestic police forces;* and *members of the various armed forces* gain a clear understanding of the **fact** that for purposes of administration of government services on American State soil, *the* *"federal government" is a corporation with no more civil authority on the land than JC PENNY, or HARLEY DAVIDSON, INC.*

The **"federal government"** is under contract to the organic States. Our Forefathers vested *the ENTIRE civil government on the land* in the people inhabiting the land. Therefore *each American is a sovereign "organic state" of the union.* Each one of us has more civil power and authority *on the land* than the entire *"federal government"* has ever had, or ever can have.

For that reason — and as a result of the deliberations which have already taken place among other nations of the world — the *"federal government"* d.b.a. the *UNITED STATES, INC. — a French commercial corporation —* is hereby called to task for *non-performance* on its contractual obligations. The semantic deceits involved in *claiming that American State Citizens are* **"US citizens"** and all the other fraudulent claims advanced against the American people and states *are to be fully recognized for what they are* — **fraudulent claims, having no merit and owed no alliegeance nor enforcement.**

Other corporate entities, notably the *FEDERAL RESERVE* and *INTERNATIONAL MONETARY FUND,* which are responsible for creating and promoting this fraud, are to be recognized and dealt with appropriately, as *international dealers in usury and fraud.*

American Negroes have in the past been considered **"US citizens"** because that is the only *"citizenship"* they were ever granted after the Civil War, a grave travesty of justice that resulted in them having only *"civil rights"* which are only *privileges* granted by the "US Congress" instead of the *"Natural and Unalienable Rights"* they are really heir to. They were *also* claimed as chattel backing the debts of the *United States' prohibitions abolishing slavery and peonage.*

A prompt correction is available from the organic states by proclamation. The people in the organic states are granted full and *immediately recognizable status* as **"American Nationals"** owed all the *"Natural and Unalienable Rights"* of any other organic State Citizen, no matter which geographically defined state they may inhabit on the land. The only exceptions are those residents born **within** (inside) the borders of the Insular States — District of Columbia, Guam, Puerto Rico, etc. — who must *self-declare their status under Article 15 of The Universal Declaration of Human Rights*.

It has been the policy of *the United States of America* to consider all *federal employees* and *members of the active duty military who are birthright inhabitants of the United States of America,* to be temporary **"dual citizens"** subject to *the corporate UNITED STATES.*

However, *the United States of America* recognizes *no dual citizenship,* and the process required for *any birthright inhabitant of the land,* to adopt **"US Citizenship"** is both lengthy and purposeful, as stated in **US Statute at Large 2, Revised Statute 2561**. As the *employers* and *creditors* of *the United States of America* we exercise our *proprietary interest* and direct all *American State Citizens* to defend the interests and integrity of the American organic states, regardless of any contrary "orders" issued by any corporate officer of the *UNITED STATES, or foreign official* acting under the auspices of *the United States of America.*

All birthright State Citizens of *the United States of America* are specifically enjoined from engaging in any activity contrary to the health, welfare, safety, and benefit of their fellow State Citizens, or will otherwise be recognized as criminals regardless of what uniforms they wear or what authorities they pretend to have. If corporate "President" Obama should order any member of the "US military" or any armed "agency personnel" — BATF, IRS,

NSA, FEMA, etc. — to open fire upon *American State Citizens,* it would constitute a *war crime* against non-combatant civilians and it would be immediately recognized as such throughout the world.

For all military and civilian-based defense and law enforcement agencies the rule to be observed is: if you can't do it as a *private* individual, you can't do it as a *public* officer.

Any State Citizen who is forced to open fire on federally or federal "State" or "STATE" funded personnel in defense of property or life will be recognized as *a non-combatant civilian* without exception, held harmless, and supported by all members of the American Armed Forces of THE UNITED STATES OF AMERICA and all American State Militias. Any State Citizen so imposed upon by those in his or her employment or hired by those in his or her employment in any capacity whatsoever including "elected" officials, will be entitled to *full reparations* in the amount of $5,000,000.00 USD or the equivalent at the time of the damage incurred, *for every death*; $2,500,000.00 USD or the equivalent at the time of the damage, *for every permanent disability*. They shall also be owed *full reparations* for all property damage incurred and up to eighty (80) times compensatory damages at the discretion of a jury of their peers.

The individual States of the Union formed by Statehood Compact retain the full and unencumbered claim upon their birthright inhabitants. These "states" are defined geographically. They are not incorporated entities, and they are not "represented" by any incorporated "State of_____" or "STATE OF_____" organization at this time. They are presented solely by the *unincorporated* Body Politic and their individual inhabitants, who retain all organic and civil prerogatives on the land.

Those organizations currently calling themselves the "State of Alaska" or the "STATE OF ALASKA", etc., are representatives of two different governmental services corporations operated by the FEDERAL RESERVE ("State of Alaska") and the INTERNATIONAL MONETARY FUND ("STATE OF ALASKA"), doing business as franchises of the United States of America, Inc. and the UNITED STATES, INC. respectively. They have no representational capacity whatsoever and are operating under commercial contract only.

Because these "State" and "Federal" entities have all functioned under conditions of **non-disclosure and semantic deceit** serving to promulgate fraud upon the organic states and the American people, they are all to be considered **criminal syndicates** to the extent that they have been aware of their status and have failed to correct their operations and representations. **All contracts** held by these organizations or assumed to be held by these organizations **are null and void for fraud.** These contracts include but are not limited to contracts for sale, for labor, for trade, "citizenship" contracts, powers of attorney, licenses, mortgages, registrations, and application agreements of all kinds. All signatures of **American State Citizens** acting under the influence of semantic deceit and non-disclosure *are rescinded.*

All those individuals engaged in employment as "federal" and "state" and "municipal" employees and "elected officials" are hereby given Notice that they are employees of private, for-profit corporations that are merely under contract to provide designated public services, having no special status, having no immunity, and having no authority as sovereign nations or states. Any actions that they take infringing on the rights and prerogatives of **American State Citizens** are criminal acts without exception and are to be treated as criminal acts. These individuals have exactly the same standing as employees of any other commercial company, and the rules, regulations, codes, and other "statutes" they enforce are obligations unique to those organizations only.

Posse Comitatus is to be observed and enforced on the land

of the domestic organic states regardless of any Executive Order to the contrary issued by Barack H. Obama acting as "President" of the United States of America or as the President of any **incorporated** entity whatsoever. Any such imposition of "martial law" by Mr. Obama has exactly the same legal standing as "martial law" imposed by the President of BURGER KING, INTERNATIONAL or the King of Sweden on the land of the organic states. He can order his paid employees to commit hari kari if he wishes to do so, and they may follow his instructions if they care to, but they may *not* under any circumstance murder anyone, assault anyone, seize any private property, or cause any trouble for **American State Citizens**, or they shall be immediately recognized as *criminals* and be treated as such.

Likewise, the government of the United States of America may do what it wills with those who are legitimately born under its hegemony, but it cannot say one word claiming authority over any birthright State Citizen of The United States of America.

Please note that Barack H. Obama is "Commander in Chief" of the **"US Armed Forces"** which legitimately includes the Puerto Rican Navy and whatever security forces are endemic to Guam, American Samoa and the other Insular States.

The Grand Army of the Republic and its successors are obligated to perform under General Order 100.

The American Armed Forces also known as the Armed Forces of The United States of America are paid for by and obligated to serve the 50 organic states, which we represent and for which we require your service. In the absence of a properly formed and operational government of the Republic, **all rights revert to the organic states,** including the civil authority to issue these General Orders. "President" Barack H. Obama is operating as an official of the United States of America and as a corporate officer in the employ of the UNITED STATES, a French commercial corporation chartered by the International Monetary

Fund, an agency of the UNITED NATIONS. He is not now nor has he ever been elected to any public office of The United States of America.

Likewise the members of the "US Congress" have never taken the Oath of any Public Office of The United States of America and are merely operating *as private corporate officers* of the same commercial corporation d.b.a. the corporate "United States".

All offices deriving and paid and/or receiving credit entirely or in part as a result of the original equity contract known as The Constitution for the united States of America are offices of the Armed Forces of The United States of America by definition and those who serve in these offices are employees of the inhabitants of the domestic 50 States defined by Statehood Compacts. As such, you are now receiving direct orders under the civil authority of these organic states.

All the foregoing circumstance is indeed the "mischief" predicted by Chief Justice Harlan in his dissenting opinion given in *Downes v. Bidwell* — mischief resulting from allowing Congress to operate two governments at once, one a **constitutional Republic**, and the other an **oligarchy under the plenary control of Congress**. The members of the "US Congress" have been corrupted by power lust or through ignorance, subverted and used to serve the aims of criminals. That does not give anyone a license to sin. It simply requires the recognition of the sins of the members of the Congress and appropriate enlightened action depriving them of any power or excuse to continue these usurpations and deceits.

There are 515 people responsible. It is incumbent upon them to straighten things out, and for the rest of us to insist that they do. It is also the responsibility of all members of the domestic police.

_____:

Judge anna-maria-wilhelmina-hanna-sophia:riezinger-von reitzenstein von lettow-vorbeck non-negotiable autograph, under seal and in service, all rights reserved;

_____:

Judge james-clintwood:belcher non-negotiable autograph under seal and in service, all rights reserved.

Copies to:

Joint Chiefs of Staff
Major General David E Quantock
Other interested parties

10

Writ of Quo Warranto

In the Matter of james-thomas:mcbride

Issued to:
United States District Court Judge Ivan Davis
U.S. District Court Judge Ivan Davis
Albert V. Bryan U.S. Courthouse
401 Courthouse Square
Alexandria, VA 22314
16 June 2014
Via U.S. Postal Service REGISTERED MAIL
RA 393 427 525 US

The purpose of this writ is to review for the Roman Curia the authority claimed by this Court justifying its action taken against the living man james-thomas:mcbride.

Please provide photocopies of the American Bar Association Cards issued to all members of the Court associated with this case and also the Foreign Agent Documents required to be on file. Please include the Bar Association license numbers as a list.

Please describe for us what is meant by "United States District Court" as opposed to "U.S. District Court"? Are we to understand that "U.S." is simply an abbreviation for "United States" or does it denote a separate court and jurisdiction? If these are separate entities, in what jurisdiction does the "United States District Court" operate? In what jurisdiction does the "U.S. District Court" operate? In which of these Courts is **james-thomas:mcbride** being addressed?

Who holds administrative responsibility for the "United States District Court" that you operate? If it is a separate entity, who holds administrative responsibility for the "U.S. District Court"?

Our records show that **james-thomas:mcbride** was born an Ohio State Citizen on the land of the geographically defined Ohio State sixty years ago. **Does this Court have any information or documentation proving otherwise?**

Our records similarly show that **james-thomas** brought claim for his life before the Holy See after unscrupulous men deprived him of his natural estate while still a baby in his cradle. These individuals falsely claimed that they "represented" him, claimed that their commercial corporation was his beneficiary, misappropriated his credit, seized his estate, and enslaved him as chattel belonging to his own estate without his knowledge or consent. Thereafter, they claimed that he was an employee of their corporation, a "volunteer" performing various jobs including work as a postal union employee, a merchant mariner, a withholding agent for the collection of taxes, and other duties as assigned, without payment or other consideration for his work. **Does this Court have any information or documentation proving otherwise?**

It is our understanding that there are two entities calling themselves "the" united states of America and they are: The United States of America (**major**) comprised of now-50 geographically defined states created by Commonwealth Trust or Statehood Compacts and joined together by The Articles of Confederation (1781) and the United States of America (**minor**) a "union" of "American states" comprised of 7 Insular states owned as "federal territories and possessions" including the State of New Columbia/ Guam/ Puerto Rico/ American Samoa/ American Virgin Islands and *et alia*. **Does this Court have any information or documentation proving otherwise?**

According to our records as part of the fraud perpetuated

against **james-thomas:mcbride** and his estate — his estate was re-venued twice — once by a corporate franchise of "the United States of America, Incorporated" doing business under conditions of semantic deceit and again by the International Monetary Fund (IMF) doing business as the "UNITED STATES" (INC.) which removed his estate to Puerto Rico and the foreign jurisdiction of the United States of America (**minor**) described above. **Does this Court have any information or documentation proving otherwise?**

Is this second fraudulent re-venue of **james-thomas:mcbride's** estate to Puerto Rico the basis of the Court's presumption that he is a "U.S. citizen"? Is this Court claiming jurisdiction over the living man or the similarly named Puerto Rican ESTATE trust?

If claiming jurisdiction over the living man **james-thomas:mcbride** — by what right or reasoning does this Court claim that fraud is a basis for presumption and action against the victim of a crime?

If claiming jurisdiction over a fraudulently created Roman Inferior ESTATE trust that has been moved to a foreign jurisdiction in obvious Breach of Trust — by what rationale does this Court support Breach of Trust or deny the redemption of the **JAMES THOMAS MCBRIDE ESTATE** by the lawful beneficiary?

Formed as a Roman Inferior Trust **the james-thomas:mcbride** ESTATE is subject to the Roman Civil Law. As the fraud was discovered and prosecuted under Roman Civil Law and entered upon the Vatican Chancery Court there can be no mistake and no excuse or evasion related to the distribution of assets owed. **Does this Court dispute the supreme authority of the Roman Curia over all legal fictions created under Roman Civil Law?**

It is our understanding that the FEDERAL RESERVE has

since contrived to re-venue these ESTATES rightfully belonging to American State Citizens yet again, and to claim that they are now being operated as transmitting utilities under UNITED NATIONS auspices. **If so, the entire chain of fraud continues to result in more fraud.** Fraud once begun taints everything it touches, invalidating claims made at every step forever afterward, no matter how venerable a fraud may be. That is why there is no statute of limitation on any act of fraud. **Does this Court pretend otherwise?**

Our records show that **james-thom**as re-venued his redeemed estate to the jurisdiction of the air under the direct protection of the Office of the Pope and that he has maintained his material interests on the land of The United States of America (major) and the Ohio State as a beneficiary of his birthright estate and that he has faithfully kept the peace and expressed the goodwill required of him as an inhabitant of the Divine Province, which has been established as a seat of government by the Universal Postal Union. Does this Court have any information or documentation proving otherwise? Does this Court dispute the authority of the Universal Postal Union or its establishment of a post office serving the inhabitants of the air jurisdiction represented by the Divine Province? If so, why does this Court believe that the air jurisdiction is any different from the jurisdictions of the land or the sea? Why should those individuals who are permanently domiciled in the jurisdiction of the air not be entitled to the same services?

It is our understanding that **james-thomas:mcbride** is lawfully a birthright Citizen of the Ohio State having civil authority as Caesar on the land and that he is not now and has never voluntarily consented **under conditions of full disclosure and equity** to any "US citizenship" or "U.S. citizenship" status conferred by the United States of America (minor) nor any corporate "citizenship" whatsoever conferred by any commercial or non-profit corporation. **Does this Court have any information or documentation substantively proving otherwise?**

198

According to sworn affidavits of unrebutted fact proven in law by due process and standing on the record of several international courts it has been the practice of agents of the UNITED STATES (INC.) and of the United States of America (**minor**) to claim that American State Citizens (like:mcbride) have by various mistaken acts such as filing tax forms —when coerced to do so by persons representing "the U.S. government"— accepted [unpaid] employment or otherwise accepted undisclosed private contracts and thereby obligated themselves to perform according to corporate policies, regulations, codes, and other statutory rules which apply only to employees of the United States of America (**minor**) / the UNITED STATES (INC.) / the United States of America, Inc. or other similar deceitfully named incorporated entities operating in international maritime jurisdictions. Does this Court have any proof of **james-thomas:mcbride's knowing and voluntary** employment as a postal union employee of the United States of America (**minor**)? As a withholding agent responsible for collecting excise taxes owed to the United States of America (**minor**)? As a member of the Merchant Marine Service of the United States of America (**minor**)? **Does this Court have any proof of claim of valid maritime employment contract serving to justify presumption of "U.S. citizenship"?** Does this Court have job descriptions, time sheets, supervisory records, or other documentation lending credibility to these presumptions of employment? Does this Court have proof that such employment was undertaken knowingly, willingly, and under conditions of complete disclosure? Does this Court have proof that such employment was not coerced and not imposed under conditions of peonage or slavery?

Does this Court have any substantive reason to believe that **james-thomas:mcbride** knowingly and willingly agreed to give up his status as a State Citizen in favor of the slave status of a "US citizen" and thereby agreed — among other things — to be subject to the members of the US Congress reigning as kings and queens over him? That he knowingly and willingly agreed to be subject to "Selective Service" requirements? That he willingly and knowingly agreed to "donate" all his credit — savings, checking, and escrow accounts — to a Puerto Rican ESTATE trust? That he agreed to give away his labor in support of a foreign maritime entity merely and deceptively calling itself "the United States of America"? That he similarly agreed to let a foreign maritime government hypothecate debt against his private property? That he "voluntarily" contracted to accept "debt notes" — I.O.U.'s — created out of paper and hot air — "in equitable exchange" for his real property? Is the "United States District Court" in **any** plausible position while presuming **any** of these conditions to be true, or any of the implied contracts to be equitable?

What was **james-thomas:mcbride** supposedly receiving in exchange for "willingly" subjecting himself to the status of a "U.S. citizen" and giving away all his private property, even his guaranteed "Natural and Unalienable Rights" to the deceptively named United States of America (**minor**)? Does the Court claim that he received the "benefit" of access to the "Public Charitable Trust" — an unfunded private trust set up to provide relief to "freed" slaves in the wake of the Civil War? Does the Court claim that mcbride received charitable "benefits" from the "Social Security" program — which was presented to him and millions of other American State Citizens as a "required government insurance program" they were obligated to pay for as a condition of having employment in both public and private sectors? Does the Court know that these Social Security insurance payments were trustingly placed into a separate "guaranteed" fund that was subsequently pillaged and robbed by members of the "US Congress" operating as an oligarchy under conditions of semantic deceit and fraud as the separate and foreign government of "the United States of America (**minor**)"?

It is our understanding that State Citizen of Ohio **james-thomas:mcbride** is **not** subject to his **employees** and that he is owed not only good faith service but "amity in perpetuity" "friendship" "aid and assistance" from the British Crown and all members of the American Bar Association who were formerly and wrongly **licensed** to act as privateers against the estate interests of **james-thomas:mcbride**. Is this Court aware that as of September 1, 2013 all court officers became **100% individually liable** for their **acts and omissions** against American State Citizens including **james-thomas:mcbride**?

It appears likely that the Court endeavors to presume that **james-thomas's estate** is subject to the Court and that his estate is the actual object of its actions rather than the living man. Having been informed that the re-venue of his birth estate by the "State of Ohio" and its agencies was fraudulent, and therefore the subsequent re-venue of his birth estate by the International Monetary Fund and its agents to Puerto Rico was similarly tainted by fraud, and now having been informed that **james-thomas's** estate has been re-venued to the jurisdiction of the air under the protection of FRANCISCUS and that he maintains his material interests and estate upon the land of Ohio as a beneficiary — what possible rationale does this Court have for assuming jurisdiction over **james-thomas:mcbride** or his estate? He is a living man, a State Citizen of Ohio, a foreign state, and an American National inhabiting The United States of America (**major**), a foreign nation, and his individual estate domicile has been re-venued to the jurisdiction of the air. He is as immune from prosecution by the United States of America (**minor**) as a Finnish National, so we must ask what justification does this Court have for **addressing** him, much less **arresting** him?

The same acts of fraud and re-venue perpetuated against **james-thomas:mcbride** and other American State Citizens were similarly employed against the interests of the organic American states and The United States of America (major) by criminally inclined governmental services corporations merely under contract to provide public services to the victims and by the United States of America (**minor**) which pretended to "represent" The United States of America (**major**) while usurping upon the land, plundering its assets, and enslaving its people. All acts of fraud whether perpetuated by individuals or nations are similarly subject to discovery and they all have the same result: fraud vitiates all claims made upon it. Thus all interest in the geographically defined American states and all interest in the American people including their estates and their vessels in commerce reverts directly to the organic states and their living inhabitants **without exception**. Having been fully informed regarding the current status of these matters does the "United States District Court" maintain any charge against **james-thomas:mcbride**?

James-thomas:mcbride has been charged by this Court with making false claims of diplomatic immunity. We think rather that it is this Court and the officials running the United States of America (minor) who should be concerned about maintaining diplomatic immunity. **James-thomas:mcbride** is an individual "organic state" of the Union and as such exercises all civil authority upon the land of The United States of America (**major**). He is immune from prosecution by any foreign nation, including the United States of America (**minor**). Diplomatic immunity is a privileged status granted by the Global Estate Trust to heads of state, ambassadors, and others entrusted with affairs of state — including postmasters. **James-thomas** was appointed to act as a regional Postmaster in charge of North America, because the US POSTMASTER is in default and self-interestedly failing to provide the services American State Citizens are **guaranteed** by the Universal Postal Union. The UPU which is and always was an agency of the Global Estate Trust under the direct guidance of the Pope acting as Trustee is obligated to provide those services to American State Citizens. The US POSTMASTER has for some time failed to properly present passport applications for the use of American State Citizens and committed constructive fraud by not allowing them to present their status as anything but "U.S. citizen"

— that is, a "citizen" of the United States of America (**minor**). This is a form of self-incriminating identity theft enforced via monopoly inducement and inducement to perjury. It cannot be allowed or condoned by the Universal Postal Union. His Holiness Pope Benedict XVI appointed **james-thomas:mcbride** to act as Postmaster General of North America to correct this and other forms of misadministration of postal services currently affecting Canada and The United States of America (**major**). **James-thomas:mcbride** is most definitely owed diplomatic immunity in all dealings he undertakes with the United States of America (**minor**) and so are the other members of the Divine Province who act as postmasters of The United States of America (**major**). Having been fully informed of the State Citizen status of **james-thomas:mcbride** and the nature, purpose, and source of his office, does this Court continue to pretend jurisdiction over him or allege any wrong-doing related to his claim of international diplomatic immunity for himself and those he appoints to act as postmasters serving The United States of America (**major**)? Does this Court have any honest questions about his mandate to provide lawful identification and valid passports for American State Citizens or is this arrest simply more criminal obstruction aimed at enforcing identity theft and felony fraud?

James-thomas:mcbride has also been charged by this Court with issuing false documents to other members of the Divine Province. All members of the Divine Province organization are American State Citizens who have properly re-venued their estates from Puerto Rico to the global jurisdiction of the air and who maintain their material interests on the land as beneficiaries and inheritors thereof. They operate under the direct protection of FRANCISCUS and the Global Estate Trust and the Universal Postal Union as postmasters of The United States of America (**major**). We fail to see how this Court, a corporate administrative tribunal operated under contract by agencies of the United States of America (**minor**) can accuse **james-thomas:mcbride** of any wrong-doing when he is clearly occupying a foreign and superior office and responsibly administering his duties without prejudice or harm to anyone. It is his **job** to provide proper identification and passports to American State Citizens, and it is especially his responsibility to appoint postmasters to serve The United States of America (**major**) and expedite the delivery of services to American State Citizens guaranteed by the UPU. Members of the Divine Province organization operate as international peacekeepers and have individually promised to keep the peace. Does this Court have any cause to complain?

We require a prompt reply from the "U.S. District Court" and/or the "United States District Court" — whichever or both of which are prosecuting **james-thomas:mcbride**.

Anna Maria Riezinger, private attorney in service to His Holiness, Francis / Civil Judge Advocate for The United States of America (major), non-negotiable signature, all rights reserved this _____ day of June in the year 2014.

11

General Civil Orders - 2

<u>June 17, 2014</u>

Issued to All Members of the Domestic Police Forces, US Marshals Service, the Provost Marshal, Members of the American Bar Association and the American Armed Services.

These organic American states of the Union known as The United States of America (major) exercising plenary civil power upon the land hereby appoint General Carter F. Ham to lead and command The Grand Army of the Republic (GAR) and its successors under the guidance of the Joint Chiefs of Staff and with their full support.

Should it become necessary to suppress commercial mercenary forces operating under the guise of being federal government agencies including but not limited to the Department of Homeland Security, the Federal Emergency Management Administration, the Internal Revenue Service, the Bureau of Alcohol, Tobacco and Firearms, etc., General Ham shall assume immediate command and control of all armed forces and services owed to The United States of America (major) stationed in North America and shall join them under his Command as The Grand Army of the Republic. All forces of air, land, and sea are to be employed.

Any cost or loss suffered as a result of deployment of The Grand Army of the Republic shall be charged as stipulated prior.

All effort shall be made by The Grand Army of the Republic to spare life and property while undertaking any action whatsoever within the states of the Union without exception. The GAR is uniquely enabled by these Orders to operate on the land of the fifty (50) organic states for the purposes of securing the lives and property of the American States and American State Citizens. The GAR is not a foreign army and is composed primarily of American State Citizens.

If required to take field position, the local commanders shall make every effort to communicate the basis of their authority and the reasons for their presence on American State soil to ensure a prompt cessation of hostilities and a widespread understanding of the usurpations and acts of fraud which have led to any conflict. All parties must be brought to understand the nature of the federal government, the limitations of its authority, and their own obligation to act in favor of the organic states of the Union.

The Grand Army of the Republic shall continue to operate under General Order 100 known as the Lieber Code, extant from the pen of the last Republic President, Abraham Lincoln.

No orders, Executive or otherwise, issued by Barack H. Obama pretending authority on the land of the American States while operating as "President" of the UNITED STATES Corporation nor as the "President" of the United States of America (minor) are owed any performance by the Joint Chiefs of Staff, General Ham, or any Ordinary. All plainly stated grants of contractual authority evident in The Constitution for the united States of America remain in place, subject to good faith performance of the accompanying obligations and treaties.

Mr. Obama is the "President" of a governmental services corporation under contract to provide stipulated services to the organic states and is on their payroll. He otherwise acts as a foreign dignitary representing the United States of America (minor). In neither of these capacities is he allowed any granted authority to impose upon American State Citizens, endanger American State property, or command mercenary forces on American State soil — however veiled as federal civilian service agencies.

We require the Joint Chiefs of Staff and General Ham to commence measures to disarm federal civilian agency personnel and to seize control of the vast stockpiles of arms which have been improperly amassed by "the Department of Homeland Security", FEMA, and other agencies employed by the UNITED STATES.

The only federal agency allowed free egress on the land of the American States is the U.S. Marshals Service, and then only when their personnel are engaged in their duty to protect the U.S. Mail and sworn to act as constitutional officers. All other federal agency personnel are limited to unarmed service until further notice.

We direct the Joint Chiefs of Staff to communicate these first two General Civil Orders directly to Mr. Obama, the members of the "US Congress", the administrators of all "federal" agencies, the members of the "Supreme Court" and those acting as "Governors" to compel their rapid understanding and cooperation.

Any expense or damage incurred by these organic states or any American State Citizen as a result of actions undertaken by any federal agency personnel acting as armed mercenaries on American State soil will be understood as the result of violent **crimes** committed against the peaceful inhabitants of the land and will incur immediate judgment liquidating the assets of the International Monetary Fund (IMF) and the Federal Reserve (FEDERAL RESERVE) in payment of the stipulated reparations. Such crimes shall also be considered contract default increasing the public debt **subject to bounty**.

Any and all corporate officers of the UNITED STATES or any successor organization(s) inheriting "federal" service contracts who support, condone, or promote such crimes against the

American States or against American State Citizens shall be subject to arrest and prosecution for commercial and violent crimes. All foreign officials operating as elected or appointed officials of the United States of America (minor) who support, condone, or promote such crimes against the American States or against American State Citizens shall be subject to arrest, confiscation of their assets, and deportation to Puerto Rico, Guam, or such other "states" as may be willing to receive them. Such "foreign officials" include members of the American and British Bar Associations who were licensed to act as privateers against the interests of the American States and the American State Citizens from 1845 to 2013 in flagrant Breach of Trust. All such licenses are now extinguished. Members of the Bar Associations are required to cease and desist assaults against the American States and American State Citizens and shall be subject to arrest, confiscation, and deportation otherwise.

Insomuch as corporate officers operating the United States of America, Incorporated, and the UNITED STATES have contrived under conditions of fraud and semantic deceit to re-venue the estates of the American States and living American State Citizens to the foreign jurisdiction of the United States of America (minor) they are found guilty of capital crimes, including acts of fraud and treason committed between 1933 and 1945, and are condemned posthumously. Insomuch as elected officials operating the United States of America (minor) have similarly committed war crimes against the American States and their peaceful inhabitants during the same time period, they stand condemned posthumously.

No enforcement upon any American State or American State Citizen is owed as a result of any "Act" of any "Congress" operating as the sovereign government of the United States of America (minor) nor as the Board of Directors or Board of Trustees of any incorporated entity whatsoever.

208

All those (E)states and ESTATES erroneously believed to represent the American States and American State Citizens and which were conveyed by fraud and legal deceit to the United States of America (minor) and more recently to the City-State of the United Nations, are re-venued without exception to the geographically defined American States and the American State Citizens where they shall remain in perpetuity as assets belonging to the rightful and lawful beneficiaries. All legal fiction entities however structured and named after the American States and American State Citizens are returned to them and their control, free and clear of any debt, promise, encumbrance or obligation alleged against them as a result of false claims made "in their behalf" by officers of the United States of America, Inc. and the UNITED STATES, INC. or by any foreign officials operating the United States of America (minor), or the United Nations City State falsely claiming to "represent" them or have jurisdiction over them.

We note that the current circumstance is in part the result of criminal acts engaged in 150 years ago, which resulted in the **commercial** enslavement of African Americans who were summarily claimed as chattels backing "US government" debt in the wake of the Civil War. Despite every act of abolition and declaration of prohibition against both peonage and slavery, it has been the policy of the "US government" to enslave its citizens and to operate as a rogue state among the nations of the world. Instead of freeing African Americans the sum total result of the Civil War was to vastly expand **public sector** ownership of slaves, giving rise to the outrageous and improper claims that have been made against the American States and the American State Citizens that we are dealing with today. It is uniquely fitting that The Grand Army of the Republic is recalled to settle this circumstance in favor of the people.

We affirm under penalty of perjury that we are natural living birthrigtht inhabitants of the Wisconsin state and Washington state respectively, fully of age, permanently domiciled in the jurisdiction of the air, holding unimpeded material interest upon the land jurisdiction of The United States of America (major). These Gerneral Civil orders are issued apon our civil, commercial, and canon authority, by out living hands and our tesaments jointly sworn and Witnessed by Our Seals and autographs before Pope Francis and all nations, and are issued to all officers commissioned and noncommissioned, active duty and reserves, of and for The United States of america (major) requiring their service. These General Civil Orders are issued without the United States of america (minor), without the United Nations, without the City-State of Westminster, and without representatation.

_____:

Judge anna-maria-wilhelmina-hanna-sophia:riezinger-von reitzenstein von lettow-vorbeck non-negotiable autograph, under seal and in service, all rights reserved;

_____:

Judge james-clintwood:belcher non-negotiable autograph under seal and in service, all rights reserved.

Copies to:

Joint Chiefs of Staff
Major General David E Quantock
Other interested parties

ADDENDUM

FOR IMMEDIATE RELEASE:

RELEASED BY: Admin. David Robinson, 207-798-4695

UNIFIED MAINE COMMON LAW GRAND JURY
3 Linnell Circle, Brunswick, Maine, 04011
LEX NATURALIS — DEI GRATIA

PRESS RELEASE
JULY 4, 2014

ON June 19, 2014 the organic American states of the Union — known as The United States of America exercising plenary civil power upon the land — issued Orders to all Members of the domestic Police Forces, US Marshals Service, the Provost Marshal, members of the American Bar Association, and the American Armed Services; and Appointed General Carter F. Ham to lead and command The Grand Army of the Republic (GAR) and its successors under the guidance of the Joint Chiefs of Staff and with their full support.

The Orders stupulated that should it become necessary to suppress commercial mercenary forces operating under the guise of being federal government agencies — including but not limited to the Department of Homeland Security, the Federal Emergency Management Administration, the Internal Revenue Service, the Bureau of Alcohol, Tobacco and Firearms, etc. — General Ham shall assume immediate command and control of all armed forces and services owed to The United States of America stationed in North America and shall join them under his Command as The Grand Army of the Republic. And that all forces of air, land, and sea are to be employed.

Any cost or loss suffered as a result of deployment of The Grand Army of the Republic shall be charged as previously stipulated.

All effort shall be made by The Grand Army of the Republic to spare life and property while undertaking any action whatsoever within the states of the Union without exception.

The GAR is uniquely enabled by these Orders to operate on the land of the fifty (50) organic states for the purposes of securing the lives and property of the American States and American State Citizens. The GAR is not a foreign army and is composed primarily of American State Citizens.

If they are required to take field positions, the local commanders are ordered to make every effort to communicate the basis of their authority and the reasons for their presence on American State soil to ensure a prompt cessation of hostilities and a widespread understanding of the usurpations and acts of fraud which have led to any conflict.

All parties must be brought to understand the nature of the federal government, the limitations of its authority, and their own obligation to act in favor of the organic states of the Union.

The Grand Army of the Republic (GAR) shall continue to operate under General Order 100 known as the Lieber Code, extant from the pen of the last Republic President, Abraham Lincoln.

No orders, Executive or otherwise, issued by Barack H. Obama pretending authority on the land of the American States while operating as "President" of the UNITED STATES Corporation nor as the "President" of the United States of America, are owed any performance by the Joint Chiefs of Staff, General Ham, or any Ordinary.

All plainly stated grants of contractual authority evident in The Constitution for the united States of America remain in place, subject to good faith performance of the accompanying obligations and treaties.

Mr. Obama is the "President" of a governmental services corporation under contract to provide stipulated services to the organic states and is on their payroll. He otherwise acts as a foreign dignitary representing the United States of America, Inc. In neither of these capacities is he allowed any granted authority to impose upon American State Citizens, endanger American State property, or command mercenary forces on American State soil — however veiled as federal civilian service agencies.

The Orders require the Joint Chiefs of Staff and General Ham to commence measures to disarm federal civilian agency personnel and to seize control of the vast stockpiles of arms which have been improperly amassed by "the Department of Homeland Security", FEMA, and other agencies employed by the UNITED STATES.

The only federal agency allowed free egress on the land of the American States is the U.S. Marshals Service, and then only when their personnel are engaged in their duty to protect the U.S. Mail and sworn to act as constitutional officers. All other federal agency personnel are limited to unarmed service until further notice.

The Joint Chiefs of Staff are directed to communicate these General Civil Orders directly to Mr. Obama, the members of the "US Congress", the administrators of all "federal" agencies, the members of the "Supreme Court" and those acting as "Governors" to compel their rapid understanding and cooperation.

Any expense or damage incurred by these organic states or any American State Citizen as a result of actions undertaken by any federal agency personnel acting as armed mercenaries on American State soil will be understood as the result of violent **crimes** committed against the peaceful inhabitants of the land and will incur immediate judgment liquidating the assets of the International Monetary Fund (IMF) and the Federal Reserve (FEDERAL RESERVE) in payment of the stipulated reparations. Such crimes shall also be considered contract default increasing the public debt **subject to bounty**.

Any and all corporate officers of the UNITED STATES or any successor organization(s) inheriting "federal" service contracts who support, condone, or promote such crimes against the American States or against American State Citizens shall be subject to arrest and prosecution for commercial and violent crimes.

All foreign officials operating as elected or appointed officials of the United States of America (minor) who support, condone, or promote such crimes against the American States or against American State Citizens shall be subject to arrest, confiscation of their assets, and deportation to Puerto Rico, Guam, or such other "states" as may be willing to receive them.

Such "foreign officials" include members of the American and British Bar Associations who were licensed to act as privateers against the interests of the American States and the American State Citizens from 1845 to 2013 in flagrant Breach of Trust. **All such licenses are now extinguished.** Members of the Bar Associations are required to cease and desist assaults against the American States and American State Citizens and shall be subject to arrest, confiscation, and deportation otherwise.

Insomuch as corporate officers operating the United States of America, Incorporated, and the UNITED STATES have contrived under conditions of fraud and semantic deceit to re-venue the estates of the American States and living American State Citizens to the foreign jurisdiction of the United States of America (minor) they are found guilty of capital crimes, including acts of fraud and treason committed between 1933 and 1945, and are condemned posthumously. Insomuch as elected officials operating the United States of America (minor) have similarly committed war crimes against the American States and their peaceful inhabitants during the same time period, they stand condemned posthumously.

No enforcement upon any American State or American State Citizen is owed as a result of any "Act" of any "Congress" operating as the sovereign government of the United States of America (minor) nor as the Board of Directors or Board of Trustees of any incorporated entity whatsoever.

All those (E)states and ESTATES erroneously believed to represent the American States and American State Citizens and which were conveyed by fraud and legal deceit to the United States of America (minor) and more recently to the City-State of the United Nations, are re-venued without exception to the geographically defined American States and the American State Citizens where they shall remain in perpetuity as assets belonging to the rightful and lawful beneficiaries.

All legal fiction entities however structured and named after the American States and American State Citizens are returned to them and their control, free and clear of any debt, promise, encumbrance or obligation alleged against them as a result of false claims made "in their behalf" by officers of the United States of America, Inc. and the UNITED STATES, INC. or by any foreign officials operating the United States of America (minor), or the United Nations City State falsely claiming to "represent" them or have jurisdiction over them.

The current circumstance is in part the result of criminal acts engaged in 150 years ago, which resulted in the **commercial** enslavement of African Americans who were summarily claimed as chattels backing "US government" debt in the wake of the Civil War. Despite every act of abolition and declaration of prohibition against both peonage and slavery, it has been the policy of the "US government" to enslave its citizens and to operate as a rogue state among the nations of the world.

Instead of freeing African Americans the sum total result of the Civil War was to vastly expand **public sector** ownership of slaves, giving rise to the outrageous and improper claims that have been made against the American States and the American State Citizens that we are dealing with today.

It is uniquely fitting that The Grand Army of the Republic is recalled to settle this circumstance in favor of the people.

These Orders were addressed to and received by:

Joint Chief of Staff
9999 Joint Staff
Pentagon
Washington, DC 20318 - 9999

US Postal Service CERTIFIED MAIL RECEIPT
7012 3460 0003 4344 3512   JUN 19 2014

For a more detailed report read:
DISCLOSURE 101: What You Need To Know
https://www.createspace.com/4870915

What? Civil War???

They've seriously "over-interpreted" the situation, don't you think? Civil War???

We have given the Joint Chiefs the right and the obligation to act in behalf of the civil powers of the states to re-commission the Grand Army of the Republic (our army) to defend American States and American State Citizens. We have instructed them to commence the organizational and diplomatic process needed to secure peaceful disarmament of the various federal agencies that have been improperly developed as private commercial armies on American soil.

That is not the "same as" any declaration of Civil War. It's more like a declaration of . . . we know who we are, we know who is under contract to defend our security interests, and we know what Obama has been doing . . . so we just pre-empted him and pulled rank. The employer is always greater than the employee.

Although we face a very real national security threat, derailing it is more of a detente issue than anything else — hopefully. So long as Mr. Obama's authority to command any military action within the several states is disallowed and the real Army is enabled to lawfully act on our behalf, there is very little chance that mercenaries will be deployed because (1) we placed humongous commercial liens against the perpetrators and specifically identified them, so they can't profit from their misdeeds no matter what they do, and (2) they would be facing both the regular U.S. Army and the American People in an outrageously and obviously criminal action — no false flag they fly now will have credibility, because everyone will recognize it for what it is.

Next on the list, is to prevent the IMF from seizing American bank assets. They are poised to do this via the strawman's name on the accounts. We need to freeze them out in a big way. We are well on our way to combining what we have learned with Tim Turner's first blush attempt to deliver a knock out punch in Admiralty jurisdiction, and then go after the bankers directly. We need thousands of people nationwide to file some paperwork and send a letter to Christine LaGrande, the IMF boss, to likewise let the IMF know that we know who we are; to whom the money is owed; etc.

Certified letter confirmed by USPS

Yes, it came from Wasilla, Alaska. The people who drafted and sent the **General Civil Orders** to the Joint Chiefs of Staff inhabit the Alaska state.

We do have absolute sovereignty when we exercise it. When we exercise an office and **"demean" ourselves** to do so, taking on **all the liability of office,** we obligate ourselves via affirmations made to exercise that office **with complete liability** for our actions. If we should prove false to the duty we undertake, we could — if the transgression is serious — be imprisoned, fined, or even executed **for treason.** So it is NO SMALL MATTER when someone voluntarily **steps down from a sovereign position** and undertakes an office—judicial or otherwise.

We have one Supreme Court vested in the Body Politic and as **the civil government is entirely vested in each and every one of us,** we are all entitled to sit on the **Mercy Seat of government.** It's just a matter of who has **guts and will enough** to take the oath and do the work and face the liability for his actions.

There is an idea — perhaps residual from all the brain-washing we have suffered — that **someone or something else** holds the authority and grants it to us. People are always looking for the source of authority thinking that it comes from the "government" or the "state" or the "voters". It doesn't. The authority to be sovereign and to act as sovereigns comes **from Nature, from God, from our very being.** It comes from the responsibility we are willing to accept. We have rights to the same degree that we accept responsibility. **Period.**

There is another idea — perhaps of the same residual kind — that the **"validity"** of our actions depends on someone else's response. Again, it does not.

The purpose of issuing the **General Civil Orders** is two-fold: to give the Joint Chiefs the **legal right** to act on behalf of the American states and the **American State Citizens,** and second, to give them the **obligation** to act.

Everyone around the world knows that the Joint Chiefs have a **contract** to protect the American states and the American people. **DEFENSE of America** is really their only legitimate role on paper, the only reason for them to exist. Now they have been given proper **General Civil Orders** from those of us who have **recouped our proper standing** and — to get to the heart of Arnie's comment —

Does their non-response in any way invalidate what we have done? No. If King George III had ignored The Declaration of Independence **would that have rendered the action invalid? No!**

If they ignore the **General Civil Orders,** they openly defy **their employers** and we are free to **terminate** all commercial contracts and **liquidate** their corportions, free to **hire** a new Army — or **rehire** the present one **under new management.**

We can lawfully **withold all payment of taxes** and leave them an operating budget based on taxes from Puerto Rico, Guam, et alia.

We can **bring demand** before the Provost Marshal to arrest all of them for court martial.

We can **fire** the whole lot of them.

We can **do whatever we need to do** to ensure the proper working of our government and preserve our own security without any apology to anyone on earth.

We can **do what we aim to do** and we can hold any guilty party accountable for failure to perform.

That is what **sovereigns** — true sovereigns **know.**

That is what **Americans** of this day and age must learn.

WE are the employers, NOT the middlemen under contract to us who are acting in **contract default** and **breach of trust.**

WE are the principals; all others are agents without recourse. Anyone who gets his **paycheck** from us or who acts under our **delegated authority** or who pretends to serve or represent us in any way, needs to **either do his job or leave.**

If the Joint Chiefs betray our interests and refuse their orders all that means is that they, like various other groups of men in our past history, **have betrayed our trust** and their sacred duty and **committed treason** — but with the **General Civil Orders** before them and in front of Obama and the members of Congress and the rest of the nation — **that treason cannot take place behind closed doors.**

The **right** to act comes with the **responsibility** to act!

This NOTICE is by my hand and upon my civil authority set this 7th day of July, 2014:

Anna Maria Wilhelmina Hanna Sophia Riezinger-von Reitzenstein von Lettow-Vorbeck, Private Attorney in service to His Holiness, Pope Francis.
In Care Of: Box 520994, Big Lake, Alaska

Anna

Four Words
"united states of america"

There are over 350 different meanings ascribed legally to the four words **"united states of america"**. There is no use even discussing it unless you know the context in which the words are being used. But, yes, the **"United States of America"** IS a corporation — a religious non-profit corporation chartered by the Roman Catholic Church, no less — in Delaware. When used in this context it may appear in all capital letters, which is one means used to identify corporations. Also, you want to pay attention to the word **"the"** and how it appears, as that often gives the best indication of the nature of the entity being discussed.

There's a lot more where that came from. I have been working this problem for 35 years, so anytime people need information about a topic, let me know. I will either know the answer or someone else in my circle of friends will have it written on their knuckles.

The whole topic you are discussing is crucial to understanding what we are dealing with. So let's take a moment and deconstruct it some more —

There's **the united States of America** — that is the Republic, notice the small **"u"** on united? That's the way the Founders designated it and the way it appears on the original **equity contract** known as **"The Constitution for the united States of America"** — note the use of the preposition **"for"** not **"of"** as well as the small **"u"** on **"united"**?

Then there is the **"federal corporation"** — the business entity responsible for providing the nineteen enumerated governmental services that the original States contracted for. That has gone by various names. The first unincorporated company formed by Ben Franklin was simply called **"The Company"** or **"The United States"** and it operated from 1754 to 1863 when it was bankrupted by Lincoln. Please note that this was a commercial governmental services company that also functioned as a trust management organization due to the two-part nature of the original Constitution.

The Constitution is BOTH **a national trust indenture** (Preamble and Bill of Rights) and **a commercial services agreement** (the nineteen enumerated services the "federal" government was supposed to provide in common for the States).

Then we went through bankruptcy reorganization euphemistically called **"reconstruction"** after the Civil War and a new Trust Management Organization and governmental services corporation was organized which published its corporate articles as the **"Constitution of the United States of America"** — note that **"the"** is not part of the name of this document and that it is not capitalized like the original Constitution, that the **"u"** in **"United"** is capitalized, and that it uses the preposition **"of"** instead of the word **"for"**. When you see any differences like this in legal documents it indicates that it is a totally different document. In this case, it is a document *peculiar to that new corporation* that was formed in the District of Columbia calling itself the **"United States of America (Incorporated)"**.

This version functioned from 1871 to 1933 when it was bankrupted by FDR. Again, we went through bankruptcy reorganization, only this time it lasted eighty years from 1933 to 2013. During that time the governmental services contract was fulfilled — from 1944 onward — by the UNITED NATIONS CORPORATION doing business as the INTERNATIONAL

MONETARY FUND, doing business as the **UNITED STATES (INC.)** Both the IMF and its **UNITED STATES subsidiary** are chartered in France.

Since the bankruptcy of **the United States of America, Inc.** finally ended, the rats have set up a **new** FEDERAL RESERVE under UNITED NATIONS corporation auspices to replace the **old** Federal Reserve System — and they are preparing to bankrupt the IMF subsidiary doing business as the **UNITED STATES**.

Then the new **"FEDERAL RESERVE"** will step in and take over the governmental services contract, and the IMF version of **"UNITED STATES"** will go into bankruptcy reorganization. It's a con game, in other words, in which these two giant banking cartels BOTH now operated by the UNITED NATIONS Corporation, abuse bankruptcy protection in a methodical, cyclic way.

There are a lot of other games being played with semantic deceit based on **"similar names"** but before we leave the topic of the name **"United States of America"** — everyone should be aware that there are **TWO nations** calling themselves **"United States of America"** — there is **The United States of America** — composed of now-fifty (50) **States of the Union** and otherwise known as **The United States of America (major)**, and there is the **United States of America (minor)** composed of the **Seven Insular States** more commonly thought of as federal territories and possessions — Guam, Puerto Rico, the State of New Columbia (that is, DC), American Samoa, et alia.

The United States of America (major) is populated by **American State Citizens**. The United States of America (minor) is populated by **US citizens.**

American State Citizens have natural and unalienable rights. **US citizens** have only the **"civil rights"** that the US CONGRESS feels like granting them.

Are you beginning to see the depth, breadth, and width of the **gigantic FRAUD** that has been practiced against Americans and the reason why you have been enslaved? How many times have you checked the box ignorantly saying that **yes**, you are a **"US citizen"**.

We all have to **stop** looking for someone else to do it; STOP looking for someone or something else to give us **"authority"**. We have all the authority in the world, bequeathed to us by our forefathers, who vested the **ENTIRE civil government on the land** in the people of America.

Representation

The so-called **"Republic for the United States of America"** is just another private club claiming to **"represent"** us, and resisting the foundational premise and requirement of the actual Republic that we each independently **present** ourselves.

Speaking for myself, now and forever, I have had enough of being **"represented"** by all those who have been elected to public offices they haven't entered or honored, and I deny any ability of the volunteer members of the **"Republic for the United States of America"** to represent me, either.

All these **"representative bodies"** seek to mislead people into thinking that these groups are the legitimate government, which implies that the rest of us are **not** the legitimate government. In fact, we are each and every one of us the **only** government and always have been. Delegating our authority via elections was only a method used to expedite administration of government services — nothing more or less.

This game of **"representing"** people has become a means of theft, corruption and deceit. We must recognize that **"representative government"** is at fault for this present circumstance and that those elected to **"represent"** us have **misrepresented** us and lined their pockets and spilled our blood. We must further recognize that human nature being what it is, this is the predictable outcome of indulging in fantasies.

To the extent that we delegate power to any other agent or agency from now on, it must be a conscious, official, **<u>individual act</u>** not subject to the vagueries of elections, Diebold machines, or "trust". We must each officially and individually choose individuals if we want them to carry our proxy, and we must saddle them with exact instructions and fiduciary accountability if we wish to continue the device of representative government at all.

Please forward my objection to the Republic for the United States of America leadership. They have no standing except the same individual standing that we all possess. Their pretensions otherwise are unseemly and offensive, and so are the underlying assumptions that they proceed upon. They believe, apparently, that when they all get together and decide what should happen to or for the rest of us, that we are under obligation to honor their will instead of our own. They conceive of the whole being greater than the individuals making up the whole, which is a patent error of logic amounting to mental illness.

Equal, means equal.

Collective representation is akin to collective guilt — an impossibility. There is no such thing as "collective guilt". There is only the guilt of **individuals** collected together. In the same way there is no such thing as "representative government" and never has been. There have only been groups of individual people **pretending** to represent others who have **not** presented themselves. This **"representation by omission"** is intrinsically fraudulent and open to abuse.

We must face the facts and our own responsibility without recourse to yet another private club claiming to represent everyone. It doesn't work. It never has. And making that mistake is how our country got into the mess we are in, in the first place.

A Sovereign Queen
addresses certain Issues

The Roman Catholic Church IS implicated in this mess up to its eyeballs and nobody including the Pope is attempting to deny it. The 1845 Treaty of Verona between the then-Pope and the British Monarch agreeing to undermine the American government that they were SUPPOSED to be Trustees for, began this whole mess.

It is important for everyone to understand that however inspired the origins of the Church may be, the actual institution is full of human faults and frailties and under constant and purposeful assault from the Crown Temple. The Crown Temple worships Satan and one of its avowed goals is to infiltrate the Church and commandeer it much as **"the United States of America (minor)"** has attempted to steal the identity and commandeer the resources of **The United States of America (major)**.

As we explain in the Final Judgment and Civil Orders, there are times when undercover agents of the Crown Temple gain prominence in the Church, which results in all sorts of evil and skullduggery being committed **"in the name of"** the Church, much as so much evil, illicit trading in arms, drugs, prostitutes, tobacco, etc. has been carried on by the CIA **"in the name of"** **America**.

In approaching this current situation it is neither helpful nor appropriate to speak in generalities of **"the Church is bad"** or **"America is good"** — because we are now very thankful to the last two Popes, Benedict and Francis, who have risked their lives and who continue to risk their lives to try to correct the errors and deceit of predecessors. In the same way, it is easily seen that much of what has been done in the name of America in recent years has *been thinly veiled naked greed, self-interest, and carnality* unleashed on the rest of the world.

It would be easy to blame **"the Church"** for not recognizing the fraud being promulgated in its name, but then, it is a rather recent development that we have become aware of the fraud being practiced against us and **"in our name"** — so instead of blaming, I suggest we apply the **"Goodwill Test"** — when you see people of whatever race, creed, political party, or other "group" — trying their best to achieve justice and peace, just skip the labels and pay attention to what they do and what they try to do, instead of being deceived by propaganda devices designed to divide and conquer us.

The Ultimate Authority is You

There is only the Alaska, or Maine, etc., state — the organic land under our feet.   Each one of us is entitled to act as a Judge of his state so long as we take the Oath of Office and discharge it faithfully according to the Law of the Land.   There is no incorporated "state" apparatus authorizing my office.   I am sworn to act as a Constitutional officer — what all these other yahoos who are PRETENDING to occupy public office should be and aren't.   That's it.   As I don't have a standing army at my back, the only way I can compel performance is the use of public opinion and moral duty and awareness on the part of individuals.   We can all read.   We all know what the Constitution is.   Some of us know more than others and are in a better position to defend our actions, but essentially, the way this country should be run and who we are and what is owed by whom is all set forth in five basic documents:

> The Declaration of Independence, The Articles of Confederation (1781), The Treaty of Paris, The Constitution for the united States of America, and your individual Statehood Compact or Commonwealth Trust Indenture.

Beyond that, a Judge is reasonably required to be familiar with the forms and jurisdictions and venues of the various kinds of law and competent to read and correctly interpret the Public Law — which I am, and proven to be by over thirty years experience.

I am sick and tired of having people scrounge around trying to find some reason to discredit me and my actions and asking for the source of my authority.   Here it is.   **Me.** My knowledge.   My standing as an American State Citizen.   Everyone has to stop looking outside themselves for sources of authority to come down out of Heaven and hit them with a magic wand. God granted us dominion over the earth (Genesis 1:26-28) and our Forefathers granted us dominion over the civil government of this particular chunk of land (See all the documents cited above.) If that isn't enough proof of authority for people, I don't know what is, and I don't propose to spend my days answering this same question over and over, and over. I have authority BECAUSE **you** have authority, too.

Is that clear enough for everyone?

I don't understand the way people react, except that they have been brainwashed into thinking that it is always **"someone else's job"** and somebody else's authority required to do what has to be done. The documents and the messages left by our Founders are clear enough. **WE** are responsible. It's **OUR** authority, **OUR** individual authority that is delegated to the government and **WE** have control over **when and if** our authority **IS** delegated, and under what conditions.

If I have a contract with you that allows me to make use of your land in exchange for services that I am supposed to provide to you in good faith, and I fail to provide those services and instead do things that are a direct loss and threat to you, are you going to stand around and worry about the **"authority"** you **"delegated"** to me in the first place? Or are you simply going to **take back the authority you granted? Rescind** the delegation of authority that you supposedly granted to these rotters to **"represent"** you, and what are you left with? Then **"PRESENT" your self**. All your raw power, all your standing as an individual entitlement holder on the land then reverts back to you and none of these interlopers can pretend that they **"represent"** you.

That is the meaning and importance of the little phrase, **"without representation"**.

That tells them and anyone else reading the document that you are doing this your self **"without representation"** — without any member of **"Congress"** standing in the middle, without any corporation able to claim a **"delegated interest"**. **"Without representation"** means you are *appearing in your native state,* fully empowered, with no middlemen and no corporate veil and no excuses — 100% individually and commercially LIABLE — and with **that responsibility** clearly accepted, you are acting in your sovereign capacity.

When a sovereign acts, do they ask where their authority comes from? **No.** They **know** they are sovereign.

Our Forefathers fully intended that each and every one of us would accept this level of authority when and if it became necessary to do so. They clearly stated that **"all men are created EQUAL"**, for a reason — and that reason speaks to the whole issue of **authority.**

A Call to Act

We all have to **stop** looking for someone else to do it, **stop** looking for someone or something else to give us **"authority"**. We have all the authority in the world bequeathed to us by our forefathers, who vested the **entire** civil government **on the land** in the people of America. Each and every one of us has more authority **on the land** than the entire federal government!

I keep thumping people on the head with this, and encourage everyone else to do the same. **Each one of us has more civil authority, on the land, than the entire federal government.** The federal government is an international maritime and admiralty jurisdiction under contract to provide services obligated by treaty and commercial contract to perform. It only remains for us to wake up and hold their feet to the fire.

WE are **The only** one Supreme Court. If you look at the Constitution it rapidly becomes clear that the Supreme Court they refer to is NOT the **"US Supreme Court"** — it is the **Supreme Court of the People** which already existed PRIOR to the Revolution!

Like everything else, the **"US Supreme Court"** is a semantic deception, a **"look a slike"** posed to create an illusion of authority vested in something or someone other than the people of this nation. **Once you know the *truth*, the circumstance is too outrageous for words.** We've been conned and defrauded for generations using nothing more than **semantic deceits and ignorance** promulgated in public schools.

"Authenticity" of the court order? We have recouped our standing as **American State Citizens** having beneficial interest on the land. As such, we are entitled to occupy any office of our organic states. We have taken and affirmed our decision **to demean ourselves** to serve in the judicial office of our organic states and taken the oath to perform these offices **with 100% commercial and moral and fiduciary liability.** That's the only **"authority"** there is, the only authority that has ever been — **the right to act resides in the responsibility accepted.**

It's origination comes of and from who we all are. **All of us.** And the equal realization that **we have all been defrauded and abused** by our hired **"servants".**

Quite literally, the butlers and the housemaids have stolen our credit cards and thrown the beneficiaries out of the house. They've hired and equipped armies to use against us by spending **our misappropriated credit** toward this end. The further origination comes from knowing that **the banking cabals and the "US government"** <u>owe us,</u> **the American people, a tremendous amount of money** — both actual cash value and misappropriated credit — and **now that, that debt is due** they wish to **kill their creditors,** and propose to **make a profit off murdering us** by taking out **million dollar life insurance polices** on every American man, woman, and child.

Their intent is **obvious** and has been obvious for months and both the American intelligence community and the Army have been **ordered to stand down** by Mr. Obama, a corporate "President" who has only been elected to the "Presidency" of the **UNITED STATES Corporation** and the "Presidency" of **"the United States of America (Minor)"** comprised of the "American" "states" of Guam, Puerto Rico, American Samoa... **the Seven so-called Insular states.**

Obama is not now and **never has been** elected to ANY office representing **The United States of America (major)** — **the 50 states.** People have **got** to understand this and exercise their own power. Our **ship of state** is adrift and headed for the rocks because **the American people are not at the helm** — are not exercising their own authority and are not accepting their own responsibility — **aren't even recognizing who they are.**

Now, some of us have awakened and done the things necessary to **redeclare our identity and standing** and acting as the lawful beneficiaries **demeaning ourselves to accept judicial office** and take the oath, sitting in judgment of this situation.

As the **true employers** and **entitlement holders** of our Armed Forces, we have both the **right** and the **responsibility,** acting in our own behalf, to give orders to the Joint Chiefs of Staff; and **if they fail us their betrayal and treason will stand before the nation . . . and the entire world.**

If **Mr. Obama** thinks that he is going to order the DHS or FEMA or any of these other so-called **"government agencies"** to operate as **commercial mercenary armies** on American soil against the American people without it being **exposed to the entire world as a criminal enterprise** — he had better think again. Even the people working for these agencies are going to know — up front — what **these banking cabals** are proposing to do and what the **"US government"** has colluded with the banking interests, to do.

Examine those **General Civil Orders** more carefully and you will notice some pecular things. **First, they operate on two levels.** On one level, they require that **posse comitatus be maintained,** and then on the other hand they require that **The Grand Army of the Republic be <u>re-commissioned</u>: OUR ARMY.**

This is to **put it plainly to the Joint Chiefs,** that modern armies of **OTHER** nations, such as NATO forces or UN forces, **are NOT allowed egress on American state soil.** Only our **OWN** Army, **The Grand Army of the Republic,** is allowed to bypass **posse comitatus** for the restricted purpose of **protecting**

the interests of the American states, and the American State Citizens.

You will also note that *commercial stipulations* are put in place — these function as **contracts.** The vermin responsible for **this threat to our "national security"** have taken out huge life insurance policies on every American; and We have placed **huge commercial liens** against them in reply — **five million per American killed, — plus other damages.** We've taken the profit out of the scenario — **Zero, Zilch.**

As for my husband and I, we are what is lightly discussed in the **"Answers" part** of the **Final Judgment and Civil Orders: — Shepherds.** We are here to **defend the sheep with our lives, our fortunes, and our sacred honor.**

We are called to duty and labor in Christ, and by **ancient obligation to the Christian Church as a whole. We are "temporal officers" charged with oversight.** Even if we were not **Americans** (though we are by birth right State Citizens of Wisconsin and Washington states) — having become aware of such outrageous fraud, theft, and now, reckless endangerment and self-interested murder planned against innocent people — **we act as canon judges.**

We levy **the full weight of God's Judgment:** *"where two or more are gathered"* and *"shake the dust from your feet".* That is why **we issued the orders using our canon names.** Our **civil authority** derives from our **reclaimed birthright status** as American State Citizens. Our **commercial authority** comes from **our right to contract** and our **100% liability.**

At the end of the day, **the only "laws" are the 'Law of Love'** and **the 'Law of Free Will',** in the operation of canon law. We have exercised **both** to intervene in behalf of the **American states and the American people.** The 'Law of Love' **protects the lives and peace of the innocent.** The

'Law of Free Will', **we exercise,** in dictating our **Orders to the Joint Chiefs of Staff.** Prior to this we went through the entire **Due Process requirements** to additionally render the rats in **complete, admitted, commercial and administrative dishonor and default** (commercial authority).

Our right to act as **Judges *at canon law*** derives from our devotion to Christ and His Sheep;

Our right to act as **Judges *of state*** derives from our identity as **organic "states" of the Union** and **birthright State Citizens** of the Union States;

Our right to act as **Judges *in commerce*** derives from the **Due Process** given to all parties concerned;

Notice upon Notice, upon Notice; Witnessed and Verified.

Our right to act **Finally** rests upon our **willingness to take the oath of office and accept full responsibility for our actions.**

Is there anyone who cares to claim that we do *NOT* have the right, ability, and responsibility to direct our employees as to our Desire and our Will, for their service to protect our material interests and safety?

Think about it all for five minutes. **Mr. Obama is the "President"** of a *foreign corporation* **under contract to SERVE us.** He is also the **"President"** of a *foreign nation* calling itself **"the United States of America (minor)".**

And we are **all** standing around **letting him threaten and endanger our lives** by buying billions of rounds of ammunition and using **our credit** to buy tanks and armored vehicles and explosives to use on American soil and to build FEMA camps and **hire mercenaries** to kill us. **Hello? Without a peep?** We are letting banks establish **monopoly control** of our money and **forcing us to use I.O.U.'s** instead of lawful money as currency, so that we are automatically forced **into unending perpetual debt** for NO REASON but stupidity? Hello, hello, hello...?

We are putting up with this *without* **an effective objection**??? Without countermanding our **SERVANTS**??? Hello??? It's one thing to be sheep, and another to be Shepherds it's true, but **there are many, many Shepherds called to guard the flock.**

The so-called **"government"** in this case is nothing but a **for-profit, mostly *foreign-owned* commercial corporation** d.b.a. **"UNITED STATES"** chartered with the rest of the IMF, **in France,** which has acted in **gross breach of contract and trust.** It deserves and gets no respect it doesn't earn.

And the only **"United States of America"** currently functioning, as a sovereign nation, is the **puny, insignificant mutant phony "nation" made up of the "Seven Insular States"** more normally thought of as **"federal territories and possessions"** improperly and fraudulently operating as **"the United States of America (minor)"** — the "federal zone".

It is time for the states and the people of **The United States of America (major)** to stand up and speak. It's time for us to **hold their feet to the flames,** to expose the corruption, nature, and identity of the FRAUD that has been used to **steal our national identity and rob us blind** and now threatens to endanger the peace and our very lives.

Instead of standing around wondering what **the writers' of the orders** authority is, it is high time for men and women throughout this country **to realize what *THEIR* authority is** and their *absolute authority* **to demand SERVICE from their PUBLIC SERVANTS and to defend their own interests and lives** against these interloping crime syndicates operating on our shores **in flagrant violation of commercial contract, treaty, and trust.**

If the Joint Chiefs don't **willingly, happily, and quickly act in favor of the people,** *their actual employers,* and don't recognize that **their primary and only duty is to protect the people of these Several states, and the resources of these organic states,** then they need to be recognized as **Traitors.**

Their **Treason** needs to be **on the record before the whole world.** And they need to be <u>**replaced by men**</u> who will honor their obligations.

That was, and is our purpose, decision, and intent.

————————————————————————**:**

Judge *anna-maria-wilhelmina-hanna-sophia: riezinger-von reitzenstein von lettow-vorbeck* **non-negotiable autograph, under seal, in service to the people and the Pope, all rights reserved;**

————————————————————————**:**

Judge *james-clintwood:belcher* **non-negotiable autograph under seal, in service to the people and the Pope, all rights reserved.**

Final Judgment and Civil Orders
Background

Final Judgment and Civil Orders
Background — A visit with Anna

If you think you learned a lot from other things I have shared, take the time to read the **Final Judgment**. The first section of the document, the actual **"Judgment"** is boring and legalistic, especially if you don't know the full detail of all that has gone on and why each section of it is important. The second section which answers questions is *what you need to read and understand*. It gives you the low down of how they operate, some of the important mechanisms they use to steal from the populace, what motivates them, why the current situation is intolerable....

Armed with this new understanding, you will be much better prepared and enabled to look around the corners. Once people get the hang of the other side's *method of operating* it will be much easier for them to recognize the criminality of **"their" government**. Simply recognizing the problem with clarity and knowing that it exists is *the first step* toward finding solutions. Knowing the history of the fraud gives you the confidence to proceed on solid ground. Most of all, *knowing who you are* and what your role is absolutely vital. So long as Americans remain mired in questions about their own authority and ability to act, they are *paralyzed* like deer in the headlights.

With a common understanding of who **"We, the People"** are, we naturally move forward without coordination. This is also part of the beauty of the **Founding Concept**.

Once people realize that they are sovereign, they are empowered to act and to choose what seems best to them.

As a self-interested group, the vast majority of us agree on basic concepts like honest courts and respect for our natural rights, so as millions of Americans take up the work before them, there is an astonishing **"common thread"** running through all the raindrop-like individual actions. The Will of the People gets expressed. The **"government"** is then forced to listen.

This present system of **"representative government"** has never worked well — largely because it is impossible for anyone to truly **present** anyone else. When we don't **"show up"** and govern ourselves, it becomes a **government by omission**, in which a tiny number of people **(515 to be exact)** merely **presume** that they wield the authority of 390 million people. You can see for yourself that this is a patently flawed and crackpot proposition, and that it potentially serves to let those 515 people *rule as petty despots* over everyone else.

So long as **the original Constitution** was in place and being respected it kept them in check and many wise governmental **"doctrines"** were promulgated — equal representation under the law, equal footing for states admitted to the union, the Clearfield Doctrine, and many, many other **halcyon principles** were put in place to guide the operations of government. But once Congress **"got out of the barn"** and started operating its own **separate little government** controlling Washington, DC, Guam, Puerto Rico, etc., they discovered the pleasures of being **plenary oligarchs** instead of constitutionally empowered **"representatives"**.

This entire situation derives directly from the US Congress **malfunctioning and scheming up** ways to entrap otherwise free people into their **"municipal"** dominion, where they could use them as slaves and claim their assets as collateral backing the credit cards of the **members of Congress**. The problem, to put it another way, is that **"the United States of America (minor)"** — **the corporate UNITED STATES** — composed of the

"**American**" "**states**" **of** "**New Columbia**" (what they've called DC since 1984), Guam, Puerto Rico, et alia — should not exist, should not be named anything so similar to **The United States of America (major)** and should not be ruled as an **oligarchy** by Congress.

Our problem now is that the Congress has been **ALLOWED** (by the U.S. Supreme Court in the Insular Tariff Cases) to operate **two separate governments** — one a **constitutional republic**, the other a **plenary oligarchy** — and to create two separate nations with **two separate sets of law**, all housed under one roof. In such a situation, **one conflicts and competes with the other**. It doesn't take a rocket scientist to figure out that **given a choice** of ruling over their fellow citizens as slavemasters — rather than abiding by the **limits of the Constitution** and demeaning themselves as "**public servants**" — was **easier and more lucrative** for the members of Congress.

We, the People, **lulled into complacency** by being able to **hand off** our responsibility for our own government to our "**representatives**" and trusting those representatives implicitly, stopped paying attention to what was happening in Washington, DC. Now we have awakened **with a jerk and cold sweat** in the middle of the night, wondering "**What is going on here?**" Government by **omission and presumption** doesn't work. Our government only functions correctly **when we show up, en masse, and do our job**.

I've just told you what is wrong and in the **Final Judgment and Civil Orders** we've provided a "**reading list**" of primary source documents that anyone can read and investigate and use to come to their own conclusions, which we are confident will not fall far apart from our own.

We have identified the problem. We have dug out the history and **know how it developed** and who is responsible for it.

We have owned **our own culpability** for not dealing with it earlier.

We have investigated **our own roles, rights, and responsibilities**.

We are in the process of exercising **our own empowerments**.

We have recognized the **nature and limitations** of the **"federal government"** as it now exists.

We have located and identified the **international Trustees** who are responsible for this mess.

We have established that *of the three international Trustees,* the **Office of the U.S. Postmaster** and **ELIZABETH II** are in **Breach of Trust**, and only **the Pope** is responding — **as a Trustee should** — to assist in getting the **"runaway horse"** — **Congress** — back into the barn.

That's where it stands right now. The word is being passed around and like water seeping through the cracks of a barrel, about **fifty million American patriots** are seeking their own **ways and means** to address the problem. They are forming groups, including **jural societies**. They are talking to their friends and neighbors and local officials. They are paying attention to what is happening in their own **"STATE" legislatures** as well as DC. They are working together in groups like this to put together the pieces of the **giant jigsaw puzzle** and yes, they are seeing the **Big Picture** emerge. That then gives everyone a **road map** of sorts, a **common understanding** of what the problem is.

Our most immediate **brush fires** are the **economy** and the **monetary system** which our predators are working hard to our detriment.

The situation with the **"Open Border"** is emblematic. The **UNITED STATES (INC.)** is out of pocket. It can no longer just **charge off** the cost of whatever **"services"** it wishes to provide against the **unwitting Americans**, because the **bankruptcy** of the United States of America, Inc. **ended in 2013.**

Their whole **"false surety" scam** has fallen apart and they haven't yet been able to set it up again.

So, how does the **UNITED STATES, INC.** make money? By providing governmental services. What do they do when Americans are not **demanding enough** governmental services? They **create a need for more** governmental services. So they **invite millions of penniless Mexicans to swarm across our borders**.... and they **provide THEM** with services and **charge US for the cost**. If a lot of criminals come across the border, or a lot of sick people, **it's even better** from the prospective of the **UNITED STATES, INC.**, because they have to round up and provide prison space for criminals and hospitals and medical services for sick people and caretakers for unaccompanied children, and so on and on.

The whole border situation right now is a **gold mine for the UNITED STATES, INC.** They look at it as a **grand opportunity** to force us to pay for their services.

Once you start looking at things **from their perspective**, it is quite easy to make sense of things that otherwise make no sense at all.

And you realize that since this whole situation is being caused by a **private, for-profit governmental services corporation run amok**, the cost of this debacle should be charged right back to the **parent companies** responsible for its mismanagement — the **IMF** and the **UNITED NATIONS**. The IMF is an agency of the UNITED NATIONS, and the IMF owns and operates the **UNITED STATES (INC.)**. Rather than arguing with Mr. Obama or Rick Perry about their misadministration of the **UNITED STATES, INC.** and its **TEXAS franchise**, we need to send the bill for it to their bosses, **Christine LaGarde** and **UN General**

Secretary Ki-Ban Moon.

That's just one example.

The situaton with the **monetary system** is even more important to address in an effective manner. The bank accounts of hundreds of millions of Americans have been **unlawfully converted** to the ownership of **Puerto Rican ESTATE Trusts** operated **"in their names"** by the IMF. Because the ESTATE Trusts have been left in the control of the IMF, **all "our" bank accounts have been entrusted to their care, too.** This is how and why Ms. LaGarde so casually discusses the prospect of **"nationalizing"** our retirement accounts — that is, **confiscating** our bank accounts — to benefit the IMF.

Take a look at **what you think are "your" checks** and you will see that the actual name on the account is in all capital letters — which tells you that **the account holder is some kind of corporation** — a commercial corporation, a trust, a foundation, a cooperative — **some kind of legal fiction entity owns "your" bank account.** Those of us who have investigated such matters know that "JOHN QUINCY ADAMS" is a **Puerto Rican ESTATE Trust** operated by the Secretary of the Treasury of Puerto Rico and **owned by the IMF.** The colluding banks have opened an account **"in your name"** and you have been deceived into depositing your **private property** into these accounts — which the banks then **"interpret" as a voluntary donation** from an unknown source, collected by an **unpaid volunteer employee** of the ESTATE Trust, whose **"Authorizing Signature"** appears on the checks and who opened the bank account **in behalf of the ESTATE.** Don't believe it? Take out a high powered magnifiying glass and look at what appears to be **the signature line** on your **"personal"** checks. You will see that it is a line of **microprint** endlessly repeating **"authorizing signature"** or other words to that effect.

Make no mistake — your savings and retirement accounts

are **at REAL risk** — simply because you have not been informed and you have not taken action therefore **to claim and protect your own assets.** You think your assets are **"safe"** in the the bank and that there is no question that these assets belong to you, but in fact, they already belong to someone — or rather, **"something"** else — **an ESTATE Trust** that the IMF pretends to be the **beneficiary** of.

All that is standing in the way of the IMF **confiscating** every checking, savings, escrow, and retirement account in America is the **growing public knowledge of the situaton and the fraud involved** — and good old **FRANCISCUS**, the Pope, who has **drawn a line in the sand** and refused to stand by and let such a gargantuan theft occur on his watch as **Global Estate Trustee.**

The monetary system, the threat to your real estate and other assets, the commercial mercenary armies now masquerading as **"federal agencies"** on your state soil — all of it derives from mismanagement and self-interested scheming promulgated by members of the **"US CONGRESS"** past and present. You have nobody to blame **but yourself**, because you delegated your authority to these **yahoos to "represent" you** and you have **continued to delegate your authority to them** long after any reasonable person would take them to the woodshed **for more than a spring cleaning.**

So why not write to the **local Voter Registration agency** and inform them that you **rescind any applicaton they have on file** for you and that **you are not a "voter"** but are instead an **"elector"**? Then write to **"your" Congressional Delegation** and tell them that they **do not have permission to represent you.** Explain that because of the deplorable and reckless endangerment they have caused to you and your assets **you are firing them for cause.**

The **UNITED STATES, INC.** is a **commercial corporation** under contract to provide you with governmental services. If you aren't happy with the service, **you have every right** in the world **to fire them.** Do so with impunity. Write a letter to Ms. LaGrand advising her that **you are the rightful beneficiary of all assets related to the (YOUR NAME IN CAPITAL LETTERS) ESTATE TRUST** and that **you do not appreciate her presumption that the IMF has any legitimate claim to your name or any of your other private property assets.** Remind her that the **UNITED STATES. INC.** is under contract to provide you with **lawful money**, not ridiculous **"debt notes"** and that they have not done so, and so they are **in contract default and culpable for the continuing misadministration of the banks and monetary system** to which you are owed.

Slam it to 'em. Spread the word. **Refuse to pay any taxes owed by a Puerto Rican ESTATE Trust. Refuse to pay mortgages owed by Puerto Rican ESTATE Trusts.**

While you are at it, **write to the local land records office** — County Clerk, Recorder's Office, etc., — **and tell them that you made a mistake and that you should never have filed any deeds or records related to property held in your name,** with their office. Instruct them that **they are no longer to act in any trustee capacity related to you or your ESTATE** and that **they are "released" from any right or obligation to take any action related to mortgages, deeds, and other such records held in your NAME.**

Tell the local bank that **you never knowingly authorized them to set up any account for a Puerto Rican ESTATE Trust, that you were owed full disclosure, and that it was always your understanding that the account you opened with their institution was for your private use and that's why you entrusted them with your private property deposits in the first place.** Smile sweetly. Then withdraw the bulk of your credit from all accounts controlled by the commercial banks.

Open up your own private "bank" to serve yourself

and your neighbors. Use PayPal and similar services for online transactions. Buy **Green Dot** and other **Buy-As-You-Go Credit Cards.** Keep just enough in a **checking account** to pay current bills. Invest in **real assets** and let the buggers hang.

I hope you are getting an **ear-full** and an **eye-full** and that whatever else you are taking away from this discussion you now know that **you are fully empowered to act "without representation"** and that you are responsible for taking such actions as described above **to peacefully and effectively stop the predators in their tracks.**

We are dealing with **rampant "government" sponsored criminality and fraud** on an unimaginable scale. It requires awareness, prompt, effective individual action, and determination to succeed.

Get down to the bank. Start those discussions. Withdraw your money. **Keep records of all correspondence. Anything you send to any "government" agency, send via Certified U.S. Mail, Return Receipt Requested, and keep copies of it all.**

Anyone receiving Social Security payments should **write a polite letter informing the Social Security Administrators that (1) you paid for "retirement insurance" and medical coverage and you are not in receipt of any "charitable benefit" from them, and (2) you are vested in their system and grandfathered into it and owed the terms and services guaranteed at the time of your retirement and you do not accept any offer of change, including Obamacare.** Finally, inform them that **you do not grant them any Power of Attorney and that any presumption that you ever did knowingly give such authorization is mistaken on their part, and now that you are retired you decline any association with the Social Security Administration whatsoever, except that of an insured party and creditor owed good faith service.**

Thank you, very much.

And finally, realize this— **whenever you sign a document you are acting as an officer of a corporation.** Real people have **autographs**, not **"signatures".** So when you write a letter to these rats, **write your name in all small letters** and add a **disclaimer** immediately after it: **"non-negotiable autograph, all rights reserved".** When you are signing something (because you sometimes have to) as the **priority secured party creditor of the Puerto Rican ESTATE Trust**, make sure you **sign it in upper and lower case** and add **"non-negotiable signature of secured party creditor, all rights reserved"** or words to that effect.

If you have to correspond with the **Internal Revenue Service** (run by the FEDERAL RESERVE) or with the **"IRS"** (run by the IMF) — make sure to **get everything in writing, never offer to talk with any of their agents.** These are **private** bill collectors working for the equally **private** governmental services company, and they are both **working off different "sides" of the Puerto Rican ESTATE Trust.**

The **"Internal Revenue Service"** holds the **credit side** of **"your" ESTATE's trust account** under **"your" Social Security Number** being used as a **"Taxpayer Identification Number"** written like this: **"123456789"** with no hyphens.

The **"IRS"** is working the **debt side** of the same account and uses the familiar Social Security account number: **123-45-6789** with hyphens.

The IRS is supposed to be **direct billing** the Internal Revenue Service and merely sending you **"informational updates"** regarding the status of the **ESTATE Trust account**, but instead, they send you a **"Billing Statement"** which you then mistakenly **assume** to be a real **Bill** because it looks like one, and mistakenly **assume** it is addressed to you, and so, you dig in your own pocket to pay it instead of telling the **"IRS"** — to **"Go, and collect the billed amount, one time only, from the Internal Revenue Service account."**

Most of the time the IRS does both — **it collects from the Internal Revenue Service by direct billing**, and then **misappropriates** the money you **"donate"** to it.

Have you had enough of this crap? Are you ready to do something effective about it? Well, its time to have a **heart to heart "talk"** with the **members of the "US CONGRESS"** and the **Joint Chiefs of Staff** and the **Internal Revenue Service** and the **Social Security Administration** and the **local bank** and, and, and…..

Fly, my monkeys, fly! Give them all back a small portion of what they've given you. **Keep your temper under control at all times, no matter what.** This is a cold business and your mood needs to be similarly cold, **business-like, determined, and no nonsense.** You are here to protect your interests and the interests of all other Americans.

Thanks to the work and research that has already been done, **you can act with confidence and rely on the public primary source documents as proof.** The rats have left a **broad trail of evidence** in their wake, and **none of it can be denied.** They have acted with **criminal negligence** and often with blatant criminal intent toward people who are owed **good faith service** instead.

AND THIS, is what the document entitled **"Final Judgment and Civil Orders"** addresses, my friends. Sorry for the long rambling explanation…. signed copies are available.

Anna

THE 10 MAXIMS
OF COMMERCIAL LAW

1. A workman is worthy of his hire.

2. All are equal under the law.

3. In commerce, truth is sovereign.

4. Truth is expressed in the form of an affidavit.

5. An unrebutted affidavit stands as truth in commerce.

6. An unrebutted affidavit becomes judgment in commerce.

7. A matter must be expressed to be resolved.

8. He who leaves the field of battle first loses by default.

9. Sacrifice is the measure of credibility.

10. A lien or claim can be satisfied only through (a) rebuttal by counter affidavit point by point; (b) resolution by a jury; or (c) payment, or performance of the claim.

Where did the Twin Towers Go?!! — 09/11/2001

The Twin Towers of the World Trade Center did not collapse. They did not collapse from fire not did they collapse from "bombs in the buildings" (nor conventional controlled demolition). They were turned into dust. They were turned into powder in mid-air.

The majority of the buildings did not slam to the ground, as evidenced by the seismic data. Nearly all of each tower was turned into dust in mid-air and either floated to the ground or blew away. The majority of what remained of the towers was paper and dust.

A gravity (collapse with or without bombs in the buildings) cannot turn a building into powder in mid-air.

The destructive process seen here in these photos involves pulverization that is nearly instantaneous, not a collapse of mortar and steel upon steel.

Bombs do not turn buildings into powder. If the two 110-story buildings had been blown up with explosives, 500,000 tons of debris for each building would have slammed down to the ground.

Nikola Tesla wanted to give free energy to the world but was afraid that it would fall into the wrong hands and be used for destructive purposes. Well it is no loner just a risk, it has already happened. However, until we can understand just how powerful this technology is, as well as how powerful the interests are that control it, we won't see it in general use.

A new kind of "free-energy" technology was possibly used.

 Debris that actually fell to the ground was almost non existent. When the air cleared, little or no significant debris remained. The remaining rubble "pile" is minimal in size. The undamaged ambulance in the photo below covered in dust is parked standing on street level and yet its roofline is higher than the remains of WTC1.

http://vimeo.com/57923364

Where Did The Towers Go?
Evidence of Directed
FREE-ENERGY TECHNOLOGY ON 9/11

Things are not always as we are told.

If you listen to the evidence carefully enough, it will speak to you and tell you exactly what has happened. If you don't know what happened, keep listening, to the still small voice, until you do.

The evidence always tells the truth.

The key is not to allow yourself to be directed away from seeing what the evidence is telling you.

Empirical evidence is the truth that theory must mimic, not the other way around.

- Where did the buildings go?

- Where is the debris pile?

- What did we really see?

- What steel was shipped to China?

- How much dust should a building make?

- Why was the dust cloud cool?

- What is St. Elmo's Fire?

Almost all of the evidential effects observed in the WTC destruction remains here and are consistent with the field effects consistent with the results of *"interferometry"*; that is, the result of interfering several beams or fields of varying frequencies of electromagnetic energy on a target zone. For instance, if you locate 2 loudspeakers in a certain way, you may end up with *dead zones* where the sound is cancelled, or *other zones* where glass and china could be damaged.

UNIFIED MAINE COMMON LAW GRAND JURY
LEX NATURALIS — DEI GRATIA

Justice and Judgment are the inhabitation of thy throne: mercy and truth shall go before thy face. - Psa 89:14

The constituted **UNIFIED MAINE COMMON LAW GRAND JURY** (UM-CLGJ) is founded on the (41) precepts of the Grand Jury outlined by **Justice Antonin Scalia** speaking for the majority in the Supreme Court case, ***United States v. Williams** 112 S.Ct. 1735, 504 U.S. 36, 118 L.Ed.2d 352 (1992).*

Justice Antonin Scalia

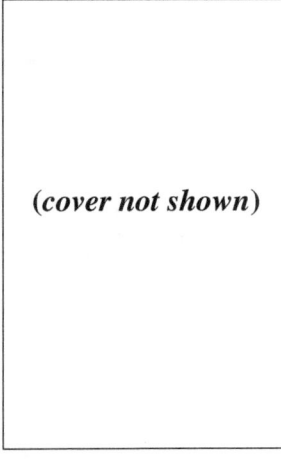

(cover not shown)

Handbook Of The Unified Maine Common Law Grand Jury For The Maine Republic Free State

Authored by David E. Robinson

"If any of our civil servants commits a wrong against any one of the People in any respect, or breaks any one of the articles of security and peace, the victim of the transgression may ask any member of this grand jury to cause that error to be amended without delay. When the wrong has been shown to four administrators of this grand jury and those four administrators are not able to settle the dispute, those four administrators shall come to the grand jury and show the twenty-five members of the grand jury the error, which if sustained by the twenty-five, under the common law of the land, shall be submitted to the court to be enforced."

    - From The Constitution of this Common Law Grand Jury

Order here: https://www.createspace.com/4711090
      (also available from AMAZON.com)

Common Law Handbook
For Juror's, Sheriff's, Bailiff's, & Justice's

Authored by David E. Robinson

"ONLY THE PEOPLE" CAN SAVE AMERICA - WILL YOU?

THEN REGISTER WITH THE "NATIONAL REGISTRY" at:
http://www.NationalLibertyAlliance.org

We are establishing Common Law Grand Juries in all 3,141 counties in the United States of America. By doing this the people will move our Courts back to "Courts of Justice" and take 100% control of our government.

Watch the video "Power of the Grand Jury."

THE DUTY OF THE "COMMON LAW GRAND JURY is to right any wrong. If anyone's unalienable rights have been violated, or removed, without a legal sentence of their peers, the Grand Jury can restore them. In addition, if a dispute shall arise concerning this matter it shall be settled according to the judgment of the Grand Jurors, the Sureties of the peace.

Order here: https://www.createspace.com/4460643

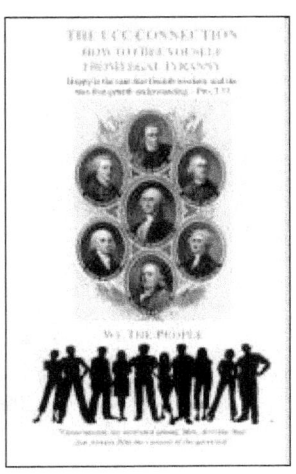

The UCC Connection
How To Free Yourself From Legal Tyranny

Authored by David E. Robinson

THE 10 MAXIMS
OF COMMERCIAL LAW

1. A workman is worthy of his hire.
2. All are equal under the law.
3. In commerce, truth is sovereign.
4. Truth is expressed in the form of an affidavit.
5. An unrebutted affidavit stands as truth in commerce.
6. An unrebutted affidavit becomes judgment in commerce.
7. A matter must be expressed to be resolved.
8. He who leaves the field of battle first loses by default.
9. Sacrifice is the measure of credibility.
10. A lien or claim can be satisfied only through (a) rebuttal by counter affidavit point by point; (b) resolution by a jury; or © payment or performance of the claim.

Order here: https://www.createspace.com/4513142
(also available from AMAZON.com)

Meet Your Strawman
And Whatever You Want To Know

Authored by David E. Robinson

If nobody has told that you have a Strawman, then this could be a very interesting experience for you.

Your Strawman was created when you were very young, far too young to know anything about it.

But then, it was meant to be a secret as it's purpose is to swindle you, and it has been used very effectively to do just that ever since it was created.

Order here: https://www.createspace.com/4466376
            (*also available from AMAZON.com*)

Chief Justice Roberts
On Obamacare & The IRS

Authored by David E. Robinson

Secret Presumption is the monumental problem Roberts has chosen to expose with his courageous ruling on Obamacare. And he did it now because our country is poised on the edge of a precipice - right now.

Compared to the absolute catastrophe of generalizing the secret taxing authority presumption, all the hell of Obamacare is merely one example, with an infinite number of the same kinds of tax laws right behind it, waiting only for Congress to vote.

Roberts also showed the SOLUTION to the problem, when he wrote that "The Framers created a Federal Government of limited powers, and assigned to this court the duty of enforcing those limits. But judgment is reserved to the people."

Order here: https://www.createspace.com/4569363
       (also available from AMAZON.com)

Thomas Jefferson

"I know no safe depositary of the ultimate powers of the society but the people themselves; and if we think them not enlightened enough to exercise their control with a wholesome discretion, the remedy is not to take it from them, but to inform their discretion by education. This is the true corrective of abuses of constitutional power."

"Educate and inform the whole mass of the people... They are the only sure reliance for the preservation of our liberty."

"An enlightened citizenry is indispensable for the proper functioning of a republic. Self-government is not possible unless the citizens are educated sufficiently to enable them to exercise oversight. It is therefore imperative that the nation see to it that a suitable education be provided for all its citizens."

"If a nation expects to be ignorant and free in a state of civilization, it expects what never was and never will be."